Contemporary Studies in Literature

Eugene Ehrlich, *Columbia University*
Daniel Murphy, *City University of New York*
Series Editors

Eugene O'Neill

a collection of criticism edited by Ernest G. Griffin

McGraw-Hill Book Company
New York • St. Louis • San Francisco • Auckland • Düsseldorf • Johannesburg
Kuala Lumpur • London • Mexico • Montreal • New Delhi • Panama • Paris
São Paulo • Singapore • Sydney • Tokyo • Toronto

123456789 MUMU 79876

Library of Congress Cataloging in Publication Data

Main entry under title:

Eugene O'Neill: a collection of criticism.

  (Contemporary studies in literature)
  Bibliography: p.
  CONTENTS: Griffin, E.G. Eugene O'Neill.—Engel, E.A. Ideas in the plays of Eugene O'Neill.— Carpenter, F.I. Eugene O'Neill, the Orient, and American transcendentalism. [etc.]
    1. O'Neill, Eugene Gladstone, 1888–1953—Criticism and interpretation—Addresses, essays, lectures. I. Griffin, Ernest G., 1916–
PS3529.N5Z635   812'.5'2   76-943
ISBN 0-07-022769-1

Preface

Like Strindberg, Eugene O'Neill wrote what has been termed "private tragedy." He was interested particularly in the fate of the person, an interest which seemingly held him aloof from immediate social and political concerns. However, this emphasis on individual destiny paradoxically allowed him—as critics are increasingly aware—to view the cultural milieu with an understanding frequently in advance of his time. His plays dramatize many of our current involvements with, say, race, feminism, mysticism, and violence. The essays in the present volume, although chosen primarily for their critical insight, frequently reflect O'Neill's relation to these contemporary issues.

Another criterion in the choice of essays has been O'Neill's artistry as a theater-man. There have recently been some lengthy and careful inquiries into O'Neill's skill as a master craftsman, and several of these, such as *A Drama of Souls: Studies in O'Neill's Super-naturalistic Technique* by the Scandinavian critic Egil Törnqvist and *O'Neill's Scenic Images* by Timo Tiusanen, are represented. In general, the opening essays comment on O'Neill's work as a whole, and the remainder deal with some of the outstanding plays in approximate chronological order. However, each essayist takes a definite stance toward O'Neill's work, offering a comprehensive as well as a particular critical comment.

A special effort has been made not to overlap with other published collections of O'Neill criticism. Fortunately, a great writer can absorb all the criticism going and still leave much to be said.

E. G. G.

York University
Toronto
January 1976

Contents

Eugene O'Neill: An Introduction to His Life and Career
Ernest G. Griffin   1

Ideas in the Plays of Eugene O'Neill
Edwin A. Engel   21

Eugene O'Neill, the Orient, and American
Transcendentalism
Frederic I. Carpenter   37

O'Neill and the Racial Myths
Peter J. Gillett   45

Desire under the Elms: A Phase of O'Neill's Philosophy
Roger Asselineau   59

Eugene O'Neill's *Strange Interlude* as a Transcript of
America in the 1920's
Otis W. Winchester   67

Mourning Becomes Electra and *A Touch of the Poet*
John H. Raleigh   81

Modern Drama and Tragedy: A View of
Mourning Becomes Electra
Elder Olson   87

The Iceman Cometh
Travis Bogard   92

O'Neill's Women in *The Iceman Cometh*
Robert J. Andreach   103

Through the Fog into the Monologue: *Long Day's
Journey into Night*
Timo Tiusanen   114

Parallel Characters and Situations in
Long Day's Journey into Night
Egil Törnqvist   130

Eugene O'Neill's Pietà
    Eric Bentley   136

Selected Bibliography   139

Ernest G. Griffin

Eugene O'Neill: An Introduction to His Life and Career

A remark once made by Eugene O'Neill in conversation with Joseph Wood Krutch has been used extensively by critics as a key to O'Neill's basic attitude as a playwright: "Most modern plays are concerned with the relation between man and man, but that does not interest me at all. I am interested only in the relation between man and God."[1] The remark certainly helps us relate O'Neill to his contemporaries, especially to those of the interwar years when the comment was reported; in a period notable for the collapse of traditional social values and for the many attempts to discover new values and social systems, O'Neill seems to stand alone, like Ahab soliloquizing on the Pequod or like his own Ephraim Cabot challenging himself and those around him: "Waal—what d'ye want? God's lonesome, hain't He? God's hard an' lonesome!" As Lionel Trilling wrote in a perceptive essay in the mid-thirties: "For O'Neill, since as far back as *The Hairy Ape,* there has been only the individual and the universe. The social organism has meant nothing."[2]

However, this emphasis of Professors Krutch and Trilling in the thirties on O'Neill's detachment from social concern needs some reconsidering in the seventies, now that the great plays of the later period have been produced and studied. For example, as a point of departure we may juxtapose O'Neill's remark "I am interested only in the relation between man and God" with the Nietzschean remark of Edmund, the character based on the young O'Neill, in *Long Day's Journey into Night*: "God is dead: of His pity for man hath God died." If "God is dead" and O'Neill is not interested in the relation between man and man, it is no mere debating point to ask against whom or what the individual man is struggling with such agony and with whom or what he must seek reconciliation. "The universe" in any nonhuman

---

[1]Eugene O'Neill, *Nine Plays* (New York: Liveright, 1932). Professor Krutch quotes O'Neill on p. xvii of his introduction.

[2]"Eugene O'Neill," *New Republic* (September 23, 1936), p. 179.

sense or in the sense in which it was adequate during the early
stages of naturalism is unsatisfying as a term to indicate the challenge to the individual in the later plays; it does not comprehend
the intensity of family involvement in the "autobiographical"
plays or the complexity of communal interrelationship and frustration in *The Iceman Cometh*. How, we might ask, does O'Neill
envisage "the other?"

O'Neill was acutely aware of just this problem. In a letter to
George Jean Nathan in the late twenties, he describes the purpose of his play *Dynamo:* "It is really the first play of a trilogy
that will dig at the roots of the sickness of today as I feel it—the
death of the old God and the failure of science and materialism to
give any satisfying new one for the surviving primitive religious
instinct to find a meaning for life in, and to comfort his fears of
death with." [3] He goes on to say that any important work in
contemporary fiction or drama must be ultimately concerned with
this issue. In O'Neill's tragic vision, there is no question that man
struggles, suffers, and yearns "to belong," but the goal is unclear
and the consolation rare. O'Neill's tragedy is the tragedy of the
very existence of the individual self, the tragedy of relentless
inner awareness and guilt, with only occasional and mysterious
moments of transcendence. In Raymond Williams' phrase, it is
"the tragedy of the isolated being." [4]

Fortunately we can, in O'Neill's world, become aware of
each other's isolation, although such recognition is spasmodic
and generally comes too late for action. Out of an association of
suffering and doomed selves emerges, paradoxically, a certain
hope, a "hopeless hope," as O'Neill expressed it in *The Straw*.
In fact, part of our "doom" is understanding and even pity; as
Larry Slade, who wishes to be the complete "isolato," has to
admit at the end of *The Iceman Cometh,* "I'll be a weak fool
looking with pity at the two sides of everything till the day I die!"
We have one other saving grace: we can laugh. *Homo patiens* is
after all *homo ridens*. Like moments of transcendence, moments
of comedy are mysterious and brief, "a sort of unfair *non
sequitur,* as though events, as though life, were being manipu-
lated just to confuse us . . . a big kind of comedy that doesn't

[3]Quoted by George Jean Nathan in "The Theatre," *The American Mercury,*
XVI, 61 (January 1929), 119.
    [4]*Modern Tragedy* (London: Chatto and Windus, 1966), p. 116. The chapter
"Private Tragedy" includes a discussion of the influence of Strindberg on
O'Neill.

stay funny very long."[5] This view of O'Neill was reflected in his technique. He considered that the first act of *The Iceman Cometh* was "hilarious comedy" (as it was, on one level, in José Quintero's famous production in The Circle in the Square), though it gave way to tragedy as the play developed.

O'Neill was, above all, an experimental writer, translating experience, in the American naturalistic and realistic fashion, into many varieties of dramatic form. His best plays are so obviously "drawn from life" that it is tempting to confuse the "drama" of his life with the drama of his autobiographical plays. His personal career is indeed intriguing. Few other modern writers have had their lives examined in such detail by expert biographers; and the thousand-page volume by Arthur and Barbara Gelb and the two large volumes by Louis Sheaffer have been supplemented by books of reminiscence. This interest in the author's life seems inexhaustible, although several full-length studies emphasizing dramatic structure have recently appeared.[6]

Eugene Gladstone O'Neill was born in a Broadway hotel situated at a corner of what is now Times Square on October 16, 1888. His father, James O'Neill, who had once been complimented by Edwin Booth on his talent as a Shakesperean actor, was playing the part of the Count in *The Count of Monte Cristo,* a role of which James was "heartily tired" but which brought him the income necessary to counteract his ever-present fear of poverty. The mother, Ellen Quinlan O'Neill, came, like her husband, of an immigrant Irish-Catholic family, but her father, unlike James's father, prospered, so that she was born into a class which expected daughters to marry into affluent and settled respectability. She was well educated in a Catholic seminary, winning a gold medal for piano playing. She apparently considered becoming a nun, but, instead, fell in love with the romantic actor O'Neill and married him. Unfortunately, she found it difficult to adapt to the actor's life, especially to the constant traveling from one hotel room to another. It was while she was traveling with her husband that her second child, Edmund, died. Her inability to forgive herself for this disaster contributed to her "chronic low spirits."[7]

---

[5]Eugene O'Neill, quoted in *Time* (October 21, 1946), p. 36.

[6]Notable examples are the studies by Travis Bogard, Timo Tiusanen, and Egil Törnqvist. Details are given in the bibliography. See also the extracts from the studies in this volume.

[7]Louis Sheaffer, *O'Neill: Son and Playwright* (Boston: Little, Brown, 1968), p. 19.

She eventually found an escape in an addiction to morphine, introduced to her by the doctor who attended her during Eugene's birth. The son—and playwright—never overcame a strong sense of guilt for being the cause of her addiction.

From the beginning, O'Neill lived in a sort of metamorphic atmosphere, one in which the facts of reality and the shadows of illusion seemed to change and interchange. He was frequently mothered more by his nurse, Sarah Sandy, than by "Ella," who had no settled home to offer the child, only the role-changing world of actors. As O'Neill was to say later, "Usually a child has a regular, fixed home, but you might say I started in as a trouper. I knew only actors and the stage. My mother nursed me in the wings and in dressing rooms."[8] The deep and frustrated yearning for a central home is frequently given expression in his drama; for example, the word "home" runs like a chorus through the speeches O'Neill gives to the mother in *Long's Day's Journey into Night*. His lack of assurance about where he would next be located appeared at times to develop into a psychological uncertainty about his very existence. His biographer, Louis Sheaffer, records an appropriately symbolic incident. Because O'Neill was fond of looking at himself in the mirror, his friend, George Cram Cook, once told him accusingly: "You're the most conceited man I've ever known, you're always looking at yourself." But O'Neill "denied it in words the other never forgot: 'No, I just wanted to be sure I'm here.' "[9]

Despite the meanness of which he is accused, the senior O'Neill sent his boys to good schools, hoping they would become respectable Roman Catholics. Eugene went first to the Academy of Mount Saint Vincent just north of New York for five years, then, in 1900, to the De La Salle Institute in midtown Manhattan. From age fourteen to nearly eighteen he attended the non-Catholic Betts Academy in Stamford, Connecticut. It was here, at age fifteen, that he made the momentous decision never to go to church again, resisting his father's attempts to force him to go. The tension, on both the spiritual and family levels, remained with him for the rest of his life. In 1906 he entered Princeton University, leaving nine months later after being dropped for "poor scholastic standing." His real college at this time was the anarchist Benjamin Tucker's bookshop. He was impressed particularly by Oscar Wilde's study of evil and guilt and the destruc-

---

[8]Ibid., p. 24.
[9]Ibid., p. 240.

tive encounter with self in *The Picture of Dorian Gray*—a story, incidentally, of metamorphosis—and, most of all, by Friedrich Nietzsche's *Thus Spake Zarathustra*. When he was nearing forty, he wrote to a friend: "Zarathustra . . . has influenced me more than any book I've ever read. I ran into it . . . when I was eighteen and I've always possessed a copy since then and every year I reread it and am never disappointed, which is more than I can say of almost any other book."[10] Not only did O'Neill recreate Zarathustra in Lazarus of *Lazarus Laughed* and quote him in *Long Day's Journey into Night*, but also he incorporated Nietzschean ideas in other plays, often in dramatic tension with ideals he inherited from family and church.

In 1909 he secretly married Kathleen Jenkins, whom he left in New York while he prospected for gold in Honduras. He did not return with any gold, but, in the few months before he contracted malaria, he received vivid impressions of the jungle, which he was able to translate into the background for *The Emperor Jones*. Ignoring the son born to him, he signed on as ordinary seaman on a Norwegian ship to Buenos Aires. For about a year, when he was twenty-one and twenty-two, he experienced life at sea and on waterfronts, often beachcombing in absolute poverty. Impressions of the teeming life of ships, docks, and harbors provided the setting for the many sea scenes in his plays and helped develop a symbolic structure for dramatizing his insight into basic human emotions, from feelings of ecstatic freedom to moods of suicidal despair.

O'Neill made another sea trip, this time to England, notable because of his association with a Liverpool Irishman named Driscoll, a ship's stoker, who not only appeared with that name in the play cycle, *S. S. Glencairn*, but who also was the inspiration for Yank in *The Hairy Ape*. In between times O'Neill stayed in a New York rooming house known as Jimmy-the-Priest's. O'Neill treasured the times he lodged in the establishment run by the ascetic-looking saloon keeper as the most exciting and rewarding of his life. He met, apart from Driscoll, Chris Christopherson who became—again with name unchanged—the father of Anna Christie; and the whole setting and atmosphere provided the dramatic milieu of *The Iceman Cometh*.

Jimmy-the-Priest's was the hangout for tough down-and-out drinkers, who for a nickel could buy a shot of whiskey or a large

---

[10]Ibid., p. 123. See also Arthur and Barbara Gelb, *O'Neill* (New York: Harper, 1962), p. 121.

schooner of beer. Not only sailors and prostitutes frequented the place but also anarchists and men thoroughly disillusioned with "purposeful" living, such as the ex-British Army officer who, in his drunken stupors, relived the battles of the Boer War. For three dollars a month, O'Neill could live in the flophouse above the saloon. O'Neill himself described the place: "Jimmy the Priest's certainly was a hell hole. It was awful. One couldn't go any lower. Gorky's Night Lodging was an ice cream parlor by comparison. The house was almost coming down and the principal housewreckers were vermin"—though the building was solid enough to last for another fifty years and was eventually pulled down.[11] No doubt O'Neill wanted to see and experience what he was later to describe in *The Iceman Cometh*: "It's the No Chance Saloon. It's Bedrock Bar, The End of the Line Café, the Bottom of the Sea Rathskeller! . . . it's the last harbor. No one here has to worry about where they're going next, because there is no farther they can go." It was as near the entrance to the tomb as he could get.

He obtained a divorce from his wife, was a cub reporter for a while, then entered Gaylord Farm Sanatorium for tubercular patients. As usual, he found material for drama in the sick and forlorn of the world—one result was the early full-length play *The Straw*—but he also came to the decision that he was destined to be a playwright. He read modern playwrights avidly—the Irish school of Synge and Yeats, the German experimenters Gerhardt Hauptmann, Frank Wedekind, and, above all, August Strindberg. Strindberg joined Nietzsche as a "reality instructor," to use Saul Bellow's term. O'Neill was ready to publish, and his father, in one of the finer moments of their strange love-hate relationship, paid for the son's first volume of plays, *Thirst and Other One Act Plays*. It received little attention, and O'Neill decided, since he wished to be not "a mediocre journeyman playwright" but "an artist or nothing," to study in Professor George Pierce Baker's graduate course in playwrighting at Harvard University. It is difficult to assess what O'Neill learned in craft in this seminar; what he appeared to receive was what he constantly yearned for, the power derived from belonging and believing, the encouragement to hope—always a key word in O'Neill from the "hopeless hope" of *The Straw* to the character Hope in *The Iceman Cometh*: "The most vital thing for us, as possible future artists and creators, to learn at that time (Good

[11]Sheaffer, op. cit., p. 191.

God! For any one to learn anywhere at any time) was to believe in our work and to keep on believing. And to hope. He helped us to hope."[12]

He had intended to return to Professor Baker for a second year, but his next stage in education was again "in the lower depths." He was back in Greenwich Village where, in a tavern nicknamed the "Hell Hole" he met Terry Carlin, a one-time idealist and anarchist and now a disillusioned but loquacious disciple of Nietzsche. In his sixties, Terry still retained his Irish charm, presenting dramatically what O'Neill needed in his vision of the philosopher-observer, a character finished with the world's vanity but still capable of grand moments of understanding and compassion. He was the real life model for Larry Slade. Such experience was fundamental for O'Neill's dramatic vision. At the same time, he never overlooked the need to study theatrical form and effect. For example, he saw the Broadway production of Hauptmann's drama *The Weavers* half a dozen times.[13]

If one wanted a specific time and place for the beginning of modern American drama, it would be July 28, 1916 in an old fish house on a wharf in Provincetown at the tip of Cape Cod. There, Eugene O'Neill's "Bound East for Cardiff" was performed in an appropriate setting, with the fog bell tolling and with the sea splashing under the wharf. The Provincetown Players moved with the production to New York, where another sea play, "In the Zone," was performed by the Washington Square Players. Boni and Liveright published *The Moon of the Caribbees and Six Other Plays of the Sea,* a volume well received by the critics, and in the year following this publication, O'Neill had his first play produced on Broadway, *Beyond the Horizon* (1920).[14] It received the Pulitzer prize.

From this time on, the story of O'Neill is the development of his dramas and to a large extent the story of the American theater. His personal life was restless and disturbed. His father died in the year of his first Broadway production, his mother two years later, and his unhappy brother, James, a year after her death. From 1918 to 1929 he was married to Agnes Boulton; their son, Shane, was a disappointment, never able to settle in a career, and their daughter, Oona, was rejected by the father when at eighteen she married Charlie Chaplin, aged fifty-four. The son by his first

[12]Ibid., p. 310.
[13]Ibid., p. 339.
[14]The date of first production is given in parentheses following each play.

marriage, Eugene O'Neill, Jr., had a brilliant academic career but committed suicide when he was forty. O'Neill himself developed a "familial tremor"—diagnosed at one time as Parkinson's disease—which eventually prevented him from writing. On the positive side, his third wife, Carlotta Monterey, was able to sustain him during his many crises and extensive journeys, and, in 1936, his international reputation was recognized with the award of the Nobel prize. He died in a Boston hotel in 1953.

It is difficult to classify O'Neill's plays since, on the one hand, he was always ready to experiment, and, on the other, he would return to themes, character types, and techniques he had used before. In general, he was rooted in the realist and naturalist tradition; his early plays express, in the form of drama, the American naturalism that runs through the work of Frank Norris, Stephen Crane, Theodore Dreiser, and E. A. Robinson. After his early dramas, notably those connected with the sea, he went through a long period of experimentalism, being influenced by European expressionism, the use of masks, and techniques intended to incorporate into theater modern patterns of thought, especially those of Nietzsche and Freud. In his later stage he returned to the tradition more familiar to him, a realism that revealed, however, a new artistic mastery developed during the course of his experimenting.

In his early realistic period his sea plays stand out—the one-act plays, "The Moon of the Caribbees," "In the Zone," "Bound East for Cardiff" and "The Long Voyage Home," and the full-length play *Anna Christie*. The four one-act plays have on occasion been presented as a cycle under the title *S. S. Glencairn*. Each play is a mood or note struck in the experience of a sailor's life, which is always subject to a fateful association with the sea. Perhaps for this reason they do not seem disconnected when seen together on the stage any more than the separate movements of a symphony. Behind all the moments of turmoil and spasms of drunken violence there are glimpses of a pervading gentle camaraderie. Symbolized in dramatic terms, a naturalistic fate surges through human consciousness, governing individual destiny in the same way that the sea surges around and ultimately decides the fate of ships and sailors' lives. The total effect, as in other products of the American naturalist tradition, is largely pessimistic, man being overpowered by "compelling, inscrutable forces behind life."[15] Yet there is a sense of heroic human endurance, of human hope and resilience forever challenging "the mournful chant from the shore" and "the brooding music, faint and far off, like the mood of the moonlight made audible" in "The Moon of the Caribbees."[16] In the more melodramatic "In the Zone," the pathos of a private and unfortunate love affair is set against the wartime menace of violence and explosion as Smitty's "black iron box" is found to be not a bomb but a collection of love letters. In "Bound East for Cardiff," the dying Yank painfully recalls his life at sea as the ship whistles and clangs its way through the fog; and in "The Long Voyage Home," the seaman Olson, expressing a constant theme of O'Neill's, fails to achieve his simple desire to go home again:

> Don't drink one drink, Ollie, or, sure you don't get home. And I want to go home this time. I feel homesick for farm and to see my people again . . . Yust like little boy, I feel homesick. . .

But he is drugged, robbed, and shanghaied, with the implication that the sea will claim him on his last voyage.

There was a "yea-saying" side to O'Neill's nature which counterbalanced the tendency to pessimism and, in some of his early plays, he attempted the difficult task of incorporating into the technique of naturalism a sense of miracle, to parallel the natural logic with a transcendent supernatural logic. For example, in "Fog" the scene is a group of survivors in a lifeboat similar to that in the naturalist story by Stephen Crane, "The Open Boat." One person in the boat, allegorically called "a poet," describes how he had decided to go down with the ship but had been urged at the last moment to save a mother and child. The outcasts are saved by the crew of a passing ship that mysteriously hears the cry of a child—mysteriously because the child has been dead for twenty-four hours. The play is not theatrically convincing. However, in the long play *Anna Christie* (1921), the destructive force of "dat ole davil, sea" has a direct clash with a redemptive force in a symbolic way that is much more convincing. As John J. McAleer points out, "Anna Christie" is "a rec-

---

[15]Quoted by R. Dilworth Rust, "The Unity of O'Neill's *S. S. Glencairn*," *American Literature*, vol. 37, no. 3 (November 1965), p. 289: "O'Neill clarified his use of the sea as a dramatic protagonist in 'Moon' as an 'attempt to achieve a higher plane of bigger, finer values,' and said it was connected with what he called 'my feeling for the impelling, inscrutable forces behind life which it is my ambition to at least faintly shadow at their work in my plays.' "

[16]The quotations are from O'Neill's stage directions.

ognizable variant of the term 'Anima Christi.' "[17] Her father's
name, Christopher Christopherson, also emphasizes the Christic
overtones, and one can follow a salvatory structure in other symbolic associations in the play. This is not to say that the play is a
"morality play"; there is, at the end of the drama, an implication
of successful marriage, to which critics have objected, but the
argument has been based on aesthetic rather than ethical
grounds.[18] In general, it was a successful beginning to the author's long search for a means of integrating, with dramatic
plausibility, the elemental forces of nature with a "super-natural"
conflict, "a drama of souls."[19]

Among O'Neill's early plays still conforming to a large extent to the realistic conventions to which American audiences
were accustomed are *Beyond the Horizon* and *The Straw* (1921),
the latter based on his sanatorium experiences. Both are concerned with the problems and ironies of "young love." Like Shaw
in such plays as *Candida*, O'Neill seems to question the romantic
tradition as a basis for marriage. In the first play the heroine,
Ruth Atkins, marries the impractical poet, who makes a failure
of the farm, while Andrew, the practical brother who tempera-
mentally had a much better chance of making a success of it,
becomes a sea-wanderer, a form of life which for him is not creative but destructive of character. As summarized, the plot sounds
melodramatically triangular, but it is shot through with the questions haunting O'Neill's mind—the ironic interplay of choice and
destiny, the frustration as well as the freedom developing from
the experience of love. The farm and physical horizon develop in
the mind, through O'Neill's technique, into symbols of the tragic
limitation of human hope, leading Alexander Woollcott to make
an interesting comparison when he reviewed the original production: "In its strength, its fidelity, its color, its irony, and its
pitilessness, it recalls nothing quite so much as one of the Wessex
tales of Thomas Hardy."[20]

In *The Straw* O'Neill draws on one of his own experiences
as a tubercular patient in a sanatorium. Stephen Murray is a
writer who leaves the sanatorium when he recovers, while Eileen

[17]"Christ Symbolism in Anna Christie," *Modern Drama*, IV (February 1962),
391.
   [18]See O'Neill's retort to the critics in a letter to the *New York Times*, published in Arthur Hobson Quinn, *A History of the American Drama from the Civil
War to the Present Day* (New York: Harper, 1927), vol. II, pp. 177f.
   [19]O'Neill's phrase in "Memoranda on Masks." See footnote 26.
   [20]Quoted in Jordan Y. Miller, *Playwright's Progress: O'Neill and the Critics*
(Chicago: Scott, Foresman, 1965), p. 19.

Carmody, very much in love with him, grows worse and is transferred to another hospital as a terminal case. Out of compassion he first pretends to be in love with her but then discovers that he *is*. The irony of the situation is an early illustration of O'Neill's tragic conception of the close *eros-thanatos* relationship in human life. Murray, who has no philosophy of reconciliation, can only demand to know why he is given such a "hopeless hope." He refuses to accept the consolation of Miss Gilpin, an example of O'Neill's compassionate female figure, both maternal and virginal—probably a heritage of the Mario-centric tradition of the Irish Catholicism of O'Neill's family.[21] "There must [she observes] be something behind it —some promise of fulfillment—somehow—somewhere—in the spirit of hope itself." But Murray cannot believe without knowing: he scornfully retorts, "What do you *know*? Can you say you *know* anything?" Like Jamie in the later play *A Moon for the Misbegotten*, he ends in a pietà scene with the girl he must leave.

Although one has to be wary of dividing O'Neill's plays into categories, since he was always an innovator and was always ready, like Shakespeare and Shaw, to absorb new influences and transmute them to his own purpose, yet one can recognize certain stages. In general, the early stage of realism was followed by extensive experimentalism. He was particularly influenced by German expressionism—or it may be more accurate to observe that the work of German expressionists like Georg Kaiser and Ernst Toller came from the same roots as O'Neill's work, that is, from the dramas of Wedekind and Strindberg. Clifford Leech takes this view and makes the point that when European expressionism was directly copied and "simply Americanized," the result "can be seen in Elmer Rice's *The Adding Machine* (1923), an ingenious but basically facetious play."[22] Mardi Valgemae in *Accelerated Grimace: Expressionism in the American Drama of the 1920s*[23] maintains that O'Neill's knowledge of German expressionism was fuller than the playwright publicly admitted. O'Neill on one occasion disclaimed the influence of German expressionism, observing that he saw Kaiser's *From Morn to Midnight* after he had written both *The Emperor Jones* and *The Hairy*

[21]John Henry Raleigh, "O'Neill's *Long Day's Journey into Night* and New England Irish-Catholicism," *Partisan Review*, XXVI (Fall 1959), 537–592. Reprinted in John Gassner, ed., *O'Neill: A Collection of Critical Essays* (Englewood Cliffs, N.J.: Prentice-Hall, 1964).

[22]*O'Neill* (London: Oliver & Boyd, 1963), p. 35.

[23](Carbondale: Southern Illinois University Press, 1972).

Ape. However, expressionist ideas were in the air, and O'Neill makes enough references in correspondence and elsewhere to show that he was well acquainted with continental experiments in drama. Certainly he used the term "expressionist" with a sense of assurance about what he wanted. For example, in the stage directions at the beginning of *The Hairy Ape,* he notes that treatment of the scenes of the play "should by no means be naturalistic," and in a letter to George Jean Nathan he wrote that the sets "must be in the Expressionistic method."[24]

The Emperor Jones (1920) may be termed expressionist insofar as expressionism basically seeks to project a subjective state through the counterpart of stylized theatrical technique. In this play the fear and disorder felt by Jones is in marked contrast to, yet revealed by, such stylized technical devices as the steady beat of tom-toms, the ritualistic movements of the witch doctor, and the objectification of the Little Formless Fears. The other characters contain and reveal parts of Jones himself, and symbolic structures are carefully developed. For example, we learn at the beginning of the play about Jones's eyes; they are "eyes . . . alive with a keen, cunning intelligence." As he says to Smithers, "Dey's some tings I ain't got to be tole. I kin see 'em in folk's eyes." Ironically, at the end of the play, this particular form of "insight" is Jones's undoing. He is confronted by the "Crocodile God" with the "eyes, glittering greenly." Jones "stares at them fascinatedly" then "fires at the green eyes in front of him." The head of the crocodile disappears, but we know it is the end of the journey for Jones. He has shot his last bullet into the eyes.

The play is important in other ways. In theatrical history, until *The Emperor Jones,* Negroes had been played by white men with colored faces. For the first time a black was given the opportunity to play a major role. Charles Gilpin made the role famous and was succeeded by Paul Robeson. In fact, O'Neill has become perhaps the leading American white author to confront directly the psychological problems emanating from the black-white polarity in American society. This confrontation frequently resulted in turbulent consequences. There was, for example, a furor over the scene in *All God's Chillun Got Wings* (1924) in which a white actress kneels before a black man and kisses his hand.[25]

[24]Ibid., p. 31.
[25]See Peter J. Gillett, "O'Neill and the Racial Myths," below, pp. 45–58.

The Hairy Ape (1922) incorporates another aspect of European expressionism, the concern with political and social change. However, it does not pursue a message or aim at social reform in the manner of the works of the German playwrights. O'Neill as usual emphasizes the individual search, particularly the inner clash of the natural animalism in man with man's own vision of a supernatural force and with the yearning for a human "home," the deep desire to belong. O'Neill synthesizes a number of experiences and symbols, including the world of ships and seamen, the black-white polarization in society, and the Dionysian-Apollonian tension as expressed by Nietzsche. The brutalizing effect of materialistic society makes man's condition apparently hopeless, yet the yea-saying quality in man gives him hope. The play is typical O'Neill in that, on the surface, it seems to follow a simple pattern, but in reality it rests on a complicated network of ironies. For example, at the beginning of the play, it is Yank himself who proudly boasts of the "brutal" and hellish furnace room and revels in the sense of power: "Who makes dis old tub run? Ain't it us guys? Well den, we belong, don't we? We belong and dey don't." Yet it is the "white apparition" of the feeble Mildred, "bored by her own anemia," who destroys his self-assurance. With a strong sense of resentment, he leaves his stokehole for the wider community in a scene in which naturalism and expressionism themselves seem to be in symbolic opposition; unshaven and smudged with coal dust he walks down a stylized Fifth Avenue, encountering, according to O'Neill's directions, "a procession of gaudy marionettes, yet with something of the relentless horror of Frankensteins in their detached, mechanical unawareness." When he tries to regain a sense of assurance and self-respect by service to the Industrial Workers of the World, he is insultingly rejected. Called an ape so often, he tries to rejoin the naturalist ape-world, only to be crushed to death. The conclusion may be interpreted as a forecast of a main theme of *The Iceman Cometh*: once a man's illusion of his self-justification is destroyed, he belongs to death.

Perhaps the high point of O'Neill's experiments with non-realistic and stylized techniques was reached in *The Great God Brown* (1926). He had become very interested in masks.[26] The

---

[26]O'Neill's three short essays on masks appeared originally in *The American Spectator* (November 1932, December 1932, and January 1933) and are conveniently available in Cargill, Faber and Fisher, eds., *O'Neill and His Plays: Four Decades of Criticism* (New York: New York University Press. 1961).

mask was obviously a useful device in expressionist drama, since
it could accentuate the contrast between the central subjectivity
of the main character and the alienating aloofness and opposition
of the social milieu. Also, O'Neill found the mask to be a useful
theatrical device in his attempt to achieve psychological reality on
the stage. He was attracted by the ambiguity of the classic mask,
which revealed while it hid, frequently hiding "the natural" but
revealing the *ethos*. He quoted its use in Japan, China, and Africa.
In his drama it could be incorporated into a metaphor for the
schizophrenia of modern man, who plays a role in the world while
yearning to rediscover the self which truly belongs to him. By
means of the mask O'Neill was able in *The Great God Brown*
"to bring out, among other things, the divided consciousness of
his hero, Dion Anthony, whose name was intended to suggest
Dionysus and St. Anthony. Not only does the mask of a mocking
Pan conceal and protect the real face of a sensitive and spiritual
artist, but the mask itself changes in time from Pan to Mephis-
topheles."[27] It was a successful experiment, the play running for
eight months on its first production in New York; as a young
Brooks Atkinson said in *The Times,* Mr. O'Neill "has placed
within the reach of the stage finer shades of beauty, more delicate
nuances of truth and more passionate qualities of emotion than
we can discover in any other single modern play."[28]

As the twenties developed, O'Neill stretched the spectacular
possibilities of theater to match the grandeur of the themes he
wished to present. In *The Fountain* (1925), the romantic but
active dreamer, Juan Ponce de Leon, seeks a mystical rebirth into
eternal life, a realization of the unity with "Eternal Becoming."
The dramatization of poetic and religious ecstasy did not satisfy
the critics or the audiences. There was a naiveté in the message
which no amount of staging could counteract; as one admirer of
other works by O'Neill put it, "A penultimate delirium of the
dying Ponce de Leon brings in through gleaming jets and dreamy
blueness as many persons as harassed the sleep of Richard
III."[29] The cry of the failing Ponce de Leon, "Oh, fountain of
eternity, drink back this drop, my soul!" does not save the situation.

Marco Millions (1928) was generally agreed to be an im-

---

[27]Eugene M. Waith, "Eugene O'Neill: An Exercise in Unmasking," *Educational Theatre Journal,* XIII, 3 (October 1961), 183. Reprinted in Gassner, op.
cit.

[28]Quoted in Miller, op. cit., p 53.

[29]Gilbert W. Gabriel quoted in Miller, op. cit., p 16.

provement in attempting to show the deficiencies of Western self-ishness and materialism in conflict with a spiritual salvation, symbolized by Oriental mysticism. The satire of American business and culture presented in the character of Marco Polo appealed especially to the critics, some of whom, however, complained as before that the ideas that were dramatized in the lavish spectacle were "simple-minded." But O'Neill was trying to say something very serious, and, although he never found support for a professional production, apart from that of the Pasadena Community Playhouse in 1928, he believed he achieved his most important work in the ambitious *Lazarus Laughed*, which requires, in the list of "characters," no less than eight "choruses" as well as "crowds," the choruses being masked according to a carefully designed and complex pattern. Only Lazarus, "freed now from the fear of death, wears no mask." O'Neill believed the play contained his "highest writing," affirming and celebrating life with the power and utter fearlessness of the "superman" Zarathustra. At the same time, although the play undoubtedly climaxes his devotion to Nietzschean ideals, in a very direct fashion, there is a compassionate rather than mocking quality in Lazarus; as Doris Alexander points out, he has the aloof, noninterfering compassion of Buddha.[30] The combination of laughter and aloof compassion causes some awkwardness in the effect achieved, because it means that Lazarus can laugh the laughter of the gods even when friends and relatives are being slaughtered. In fact, O'Neill cannot keep out of the play his own dilemma, symbolized in a tension in the character of Lazarus between love for the gently maternal Miriam, who is unhappy and pitying when others suffer, and admiration for the proud and aristocratic Pompeia, worthy consort of the superman. It is an old conflict between the Virgo Mater of his Catholicism and the Nietzschean hero of his visionary transcendentalism. However, as O'Neill observed in the subtitle, it was a play for "an Imaginative Theatre" and credit should be given for a lingering effect it has on the mind, especially in its great choral and affirmative sweep. It requires the mood of a religious congregation rather than that of the usual theater audience.

Two other plays of the twenties will probably outlast O'Neill's religious extravaganza. They explore close family relationships, one, like *Beyond the Horizon*, set in an agricultural

---

[30] "*Lazarus Laughed* and Buddha," *Modern Language Notes*, XVII (1956), 357–365.

society with characters defined largely by their relationship to the land, and one set in the sophisticated and analytic setting of academic, medical, and artistic professionals, respectively *Desire under the Elms* (1924) and *Strange Interlude* (1928). As in the earlier "farm" play, there is a "triangle" in *Desire under the Elms,* but the characters are mature; drawn with masterly realism, they have achieved power and direction in their lives. Ephraim Cabot, heir to a harsh puritanism, with a sensuality as powerful as his proud dedication to land and labor, is challenged by another character, Abbie, equally as sensual and willful in her demands on life. As Roger Asselineau observes,[31] the key word is "desire"; like the characters in "The Trilogy of Desire" by Theodore Dreiser (whose novel *An American Tragedy* was also published in the mid-twenties), O'Neill's characters are caught in a meshing of three basic "drives": the need for love, the will to power, and the desire for beauty. Yet subsuming these drives is a sort of transcendent equilibrium or fate; like an arboreal oversoul, two great elms "brood oppressively" over Cabot's house, occasionally raining tears on the roof.

By the time *Strange Interlude* was produced, O'Neill had become a playwright who could expect his audience to sit through a five-hour play with dinner between the acts. In this play audiences were apparently stirred by the adaptation of Freudianism with its "manifest" and "latent" contents, although the constant theatrical "asides" were similar in function to other devices of masking and unmasking. Also attractive to the audiences at this period was the dramatic and narrative presentation of woman as a central force, powerfully generative yet also intriguingly destructive, especially of the educated male. Like Lady Brett of Hemingway and Caddy Compson and Eula Varner of Faulkner, Nina Leeds is the focus of a male circle. One critic has suggested that the nine acts of the play, along with the name "Nina," symbolize the nine months of pregnancy.[32] Whether or not we wish to emphasize this aspect, there is a sense of overriding femininity, of "Eve triumphant."[33]

[31]See below, pp. 59–66.

[32]See Gelb, op. cit., p. 631.

[33]Cf. a German critic's review of Elizabeth Bergner's portrayal of Nina Leeds, quoted in Horst Frenz, *Eugene O'Neill,* tr. Helen Sebba (New York: Frederick Ungar, 1971), pp. 63–64:

> A brown-haired, troubled, sick girl, then a young mother who should not be one, then a lovely woman, then again a mother, then fading charms under a red wig, then an elderly lady, then a gentle old woman, and much more in the

But "Eve triumphant" cannot avoid a basic ennui. The deep and lengthy psychological involvement is ironically counterpointed with a mood of transience, an authorial stance that all is but the passing of desire.[34] As Nina concludes: "Strange Interlude! Yes, our lives are merely strange dark interludes in the electrical display of God the Father!" The play seems to imply that peace is the state of "all passions spent"; as the retiring and passive Charlie Marsden observes at the end, when Nina is asleep, he, "passed beyond desire, has all the luck at last." To this extent, *Strange Interlude* complements *Desire under the Elms* in its concern with the resolution of naturalist and Freudian instinctual desires.

The concern of O'Neill with man's desire to belong and what to belong to is developed in an extreme way in *Dynamo* (1929), produced a year after *Strange Interlude*. To use a phrase from the earlier play, the "electrical display of God the Father" is brought into a drama which is particularly concerned with "mother"—O'Neill seems obliged always to consider the patriarchal and matriarchal forces together in relation to the same problem, if not always with equal emphasis in the same play, at least in plays closely associated. Reuben Light embraces the Dynamo and, like Yank in *The Hairy Ape,* is killed by what was hoped by the hero would be a sympathetic force. O'Neill seemingly could not escape from the question "What shall I do to be saved?" In 1933, at the end of his first long productive period, some critics decided that in *Days without End* he had returned to the faith of his father. O'Neill himself knew better. His own reaction to the positive ending at the altar of "an old church"—a final scene, which recalled the theme of *Lazarus Laughed,* though more emphatically Christian: "Life laughs with God's love again! Life laughs with love!"—was typical of his mental attitude of agonizing about past decisions, of attempting to pursue two opposing logics at the same time, and of then feeling guilty for the logic he chose:

---

intervals—nine acts, nine roles, nine times a woman's love, suffering and hate-driven and driving through disillusionments and ecstasies; nine times the same person and yet another person, and always herself, with those eyes which do not need O'Neill's trick devices to say what must not be said; always with that child's face which can suddenly become tragic; always with that lovely charm which spreads a welcome cheerfulness; . . . it is Eve triumphant.

[34]On this subject, see William R. Brashear, "O'Neill's Schopenhauer Interlude," *Criticism,* VI, 3 (Summer 1964), 256–265.

"Gene would walk up and down the beach, painfully wrestling with the problem," Carlotta recalled. "He couldn't make up his mind whether or not to have the man go back to the Church. At one point he thought of having him shoot himself at the church altar, and he discussed this idea with the Jesuit priests and they persuaded him not to use it. He finally ended with the man going back to the Church. Later he was furious with himself for having done this. He felt he had ruined the play and that he was a traitor to himself as a writer. He always said the last act was a phony and he never forgave himself for it."[35]

Apart from *Days without End*, the early part of the thirties saw the first production of only two other plays by O'Neill. *Ah Wilderness* (1933) was a comedy of adolescence, representing, said O'Neill, "the way I would have *liked* my boyhood to have been." It is in some ways a modern *Midsummer Night's Dream*, a reminiscence of the delight and folly of young love played under a gentle and benevolent if somewhat amused moon. O'Neill claimed it was based on a dream and written in four weeks. Typically, to quote from O'Neill's detailed stage directions, "the crescent of the new moon casts a soft, mysterious, caressing light" on young lovers, and, at the play's end, members of the family move quietly out of the moonlight, back into the darkness of the front parlor"—back, indeed, into a more usual O'Neill setting.

Far more important was the controversial *Mourning Becomes Electra* (1931), the most direct use of the pattern of Greek tragedy in O'Neill. The long trilogy has been repeatedly compared, as it was bound to be, with the Aeschylean cycle, usually unfavorably.[36] O'Neill himself tussled with the problem of bringing the Greek myth into modern times.[37] Paradoxically, we may perhaps see the play cycle in a better light if we view it historically in relation to the Civil War period and to the psychology of puritanism.[38] O'Neill echoes in his characters the classical names (for example, Ezra Mannon for Agamemnon) and follows the movement of the classic trilogy in his three plays, "Homecoming," "The Hunted," and "The Haunted." But instead of indi-

[35]Quoted from Gelb, op. cit., p. 764.

[36]E.g., see Olson below, pp. 87–91. Of interest on this point is Horst Frenz and Martin Mueller, "More Shakespeare and Less Aeschylus in Eugene O'Neill's *Mourning Becomes Electra*," *American Literature*, vol. 38, no. 1 (March 1966), pp. 85–100.

[37]"O'Neill's own Story of 'Electra' in the Making" was first published in the *New York Herald Tribune*, November 1931. The text is available in Barrett H. Clark, *European Theories of the Drama, with a Supplement on the American Drama* (New York: Crown, 1947).

[38]See Raleigh, below, pp. 81–86.

vidual crime followed by social justice, the theme for O'Neill is the destiny of the individual soul; we stay with the problem of self where there is no meaningful, or ultimately helpful, other-relationship. At the same time, on one level he remained profoundly classical: just as the Greek protagonists were able to practice a freedom of choice under the doom of fate, so, in spite of their fateful psychological conditioning, the characters in *Mourning Becomes Electra* have the power of decision. Like Ephraim Cabot, Lavinia is an undeviating, self-willed character, and her decision is entirely individual; she is her own judge, and she awards her own punishment. Unfortunately, she cannot, as well, show herself mercy.

In 1936, O'Neill received the Nobel prize for literature, and in his acceptance speech he took the opportunity to pay tribute to Strindberg. Between 1934 and 1946 no new plays appeared. Like Lavinia, O'Neill shut himself away from the social world, continuing to work and write in spite of serious personal ill health. He busied himself with a grand design in drama, a cycle that dramatized the history of a prominent Irish-American family. Only *A Touch of the Poet* (1957) and the unfinished *More Stately Mansions* (1962) were produced, the other manuscripts being destroyed. In the finished play the action concerns a Byronic dreamer, Cornelius Melody, who runs a tavern in which he reduces himself and his family to poverty by playing and replaying, to the accompaniment of quantities of whiskey, the great moment when he was a major in the Duke of Wellington's Army. He ignores the business side of life, while his more realistic and mocking daughter seduces another dreamer, the idealistic son of a prosperous New England family. There is a clever contrapuntal movement in the play; the themes of dream and reality intertwine, sometimes in ironic fashion. Thus when Cornelius ultimately gives up his vision of himself as a noble hero, the daughter is the first to protest at this sacrifice of pride. At the same time, the patient and humble mother reveals that she has her own enduring pride in being called upon to give an unstinting love to her family.

More successfully O'Neill turned from the cycle to the personal experiences of his own life again, writing *The Iceman Cometh* (1946), *Long Day's Journey into Night* (1956), *A Moon for the Misbegotten* (1947), and a short play, a study in loneliness, *Hughie* (1958). He returned in one sense to the realistic theater, but it is a realism with profounder reverberations than his early naturalism. He was able to view his own family and the unfortunate beings of Jimmy-the-Priest's with an understanding compassion that develops into the sympathetic and moving inevitability of great tragedy. So much has been said on *The Iceman Cometh*[39] that it seems needless to attempt to summarize the play. In general, it is a play bringing to a climax aesthetically O'Neill's basic paradox of hopeless hope. For the most part men exist through the aid of illusion. To awaken from the illusion, as "the old foolosopher" Larry Slade does, is only to realize the impasse and the despair. A few like Hickey and Parritt, caught in a web of love and hate, resentment and guilt, act in a way which brings an early nemesis; but for most there is enduring role playing and illusion.

O'Neill died in Boston in 1953. There has been much controversy about whether his widow was correct in allowing *Long Day's Journey into Night* to be published and performed, in view of the wish once expressed by her husband that it should not be produced until twenty-five years after his death. But certainly both the American and world theater are richer for having experienced, before that time, the play which some have considered the greatest American drama of the twentieth century thus far. Critics have found it difficult to interpret the play without continual reference to the autobiographical element, but recently there has been increasing study of the richness of the play as a theatrical masterpiece. It is a multiple tragedy with each of "the four haunted Tyrones" intricately and painfully involved with the other three, yet each becoming in turn his—and her—own tragic center, a human being whom the author has profoundly and compassionately understood and, in a sense, justified. Drunkenness and drug addiction symbolize a Dionysian force that allows escape from recognizing or admitting the truth, although, on occasion, it breaks down inhibitions, thereby allowing at least a part of the truth to be revealed. Through all the turmoil and intrapersonal persecution, the artist is trying to find his way to a "faithful realism," as Edmund says. In the same passage Edmund, based on the life of the young Eugene O'Neill, prophesies that he will never do more than "stammer" as a poet. Perhaps that best sums up the general style of O'Neill as playwright, a "faithful realism" rendered with a "stammering" poetry. But the stammering has its own eloquence, "the native eloquence of us fog people," as Edmund phrases it. It is the stumbling expression of modern man using the means by which he ordinarily communicates with other men to commune with whatever is divine in himself.

[39]E.g., John Henry Raleigh has collected a number of critical essays in his volume *Twentieth Century Interpretations of* The Iceman Cometh (Englewood Cliffs, N.J.: Prentice-Hall, 1968).

Edwin A. Engel

Ideas in the Plays of Eugene O'Neill

Adolescence may be a crucial period of one's life, but in Eugene O'Neill's case it was virtually his entire life—the single reality, the source of all nourishment emotional and intellectual. The plays strongly suggest this, and the recent biographies confirm it. To the end of his playwriting career O'Neill continuously drew inspiration from the dozen years beginning about 1900 (when he was twelve) and extending through 1912. "What haunted, haunting ghosts we are!" he was to have one of his heroes exclaim. "We dimly remember so much it will take us so many million years to forget!"[1] He remembered vividly, not dimly, the beginning of his religious apostasy at the turn of the century, the bitterness toward his father and the evidence that intensified it, the discovery of his mother's narcotics addiction, the depressing spectacle of his older brother's spiritual and physical deterioration, his own chronic drinking, his first mismarriage, his experiences at sea and as a vagrant, his attempted suicide, his work in the theater, his bout with tuberculosis, his enthusiasm for the philosophy of Nietzsche. In 1912, while working on the local newspaper, the New London *Telegraph,* O'Neill published some verses called "The Lay of the Singer's Fall"[2] about an idealistic boy whose youthful innocent certitude is subverted by the mocking "Devil of Doubt." The last stanza read:

> And the lips of the singer were flecked with red
> > And torn with a bitter cry,
> 'When Truth and Love and God are dead
> > It is time, full time, to die!'
> And the Devil in triumph chuckled low,
> > 'There is always suicide,
> It's the only logical thing I know.'
> > —And the life of the singer died.

[1] *The Great God Brown* (New York, 1926), Act II, scene 3.
[2] November 27, 1912.

From Ideas in the Drama: Selected Papers from the English Institute, *edited by John Gassner, 1964. Reprinted by permission of Columbia University Press and the author.*

A remarkable example of adolescent prescience, the poem was an abstract of the themes in the work of O'Neill's mature years.

Also in 1912 appeared evidence of O'Neill's abortive social consciousness, again in verses in the *Telegraph* and subsequently in the New York *Call*. He was to know individual anarchists, socialists, and communists; but by 1921 he rejected all dogma— social, political, and religious. Thereafter he was satisfied with being indignant, at times satirical, about the acquisitive spirit and about materialism generally. For the most part his plays seldom referred to anything topical. In *Strange Interlude,* to be sure, the heroine had been in love with an aviator, and mention was made of hospitalized soldiers. Otherwise the consequences of world war, of war in general, interested O'Neill but little. In *Days without End,* written during the Depression, he showed an awareness of national disaster but expressed contempt rather than compassion for the victims. Thus, he delivered a message through his hero:

> I listen to people talking about this universal breakdown we are in and I marvel at their stupid cowardice. It is so obvious that they deliberately cheat themselves because their fear of change won't let them face the truth. They don't want to understand what has happened to them. All they want is to start the merry-go-round of blind greed all over again. They no longer know what they want this country to be, what they want it to become, where they want it to go. It has lost all meaning for them except as a pig-wallow. And so their lives as citizens have no beginnings, no ends. They have lost the ideal of the Land of the Free.[3]

If O'Neill appeared in his plays to have taken only slight interest in current events or to have had little sympathy or hope for suffering humanity, it was partly because of his generally misanthropic outlook, partly because he deliberately concerned himself with timeless matters, partly because he had isolated himself from the external contemporary world by walling himself inside those early years of his life, a "haunted, haunting ghost."

Throughout most of his career O'Neill dealt with big ideas, for he wished to do what he called "big work." Generally avoiding the topical and the transitory, he preferred to treat ideas that are universal and abstract: Man, Life, Death, Love, Hate. The relation between man and man did not interest him at all, he is reported to have said; "I am interested only in the relation be-

[3](New York, 1934), Act III, scene 2.

tween man and God." The duty of the modern playwright, he thought, was "to dig at the roots of the sickness of today," the cause of which was "the death of the old God"[4] and the failure to find a new One. Without God life has no meaning, and the fear of death cannot be comforted. O'Neill dug for some twenty years, mainly at his own roots. Energetically applying himself to the task, he wrote a series of plays that concluded in conversion scenes, scenes whose ecstatic religiosity was simulated, whose fervor was artificially induced. In one play of the series he had his protagonist speak scornfully of his "fixation on old Mama Christianity."[5] There is little doubt that O'Neill was diagnosing his own condition. Had he completed the diagnosis, he would have included his fixation on Mama and Papa O'Neill, on brother Jamie, and on himself. Obsessed with the relationship between himself and his family, he repeatedly returned to the scene of whatever crimes—his family's and his own. Few writers have wrung so much agony and material for so many plays out of their adolescent years.

Before 1922, drawing upon the experiences of his sea, saloon, and sanitarium days, O'Neill had written naturalistic plays in which the simple-minded, insensitive main character became the victim of fate in various forms: psychological (the fixed idea), biological (the primitive past), physical (the sea). During this time and in these plays he occasionally introduced an incongruous figure: the sensitive, brooding, self-pitying, guilt-ridden, life-weary dreamer and, in one instance, inebriate. In *The Hairy Ape* (1922) the insensitive type prevailed, but he represented Man with a capital *M*—individually an ape, collectively the primal horde. With neither a past nor a future, Man could do nothing about the unbearable present. The materialistic world of today further brutalized and frustrated him, while religion and proposals for social and economic reform were beyond his feeble ability to understand. He was abysmally ignorant. "Belonging" (O'Neill's word) to nothing, the brute comforted himself by drinking, by drinking and "dope-dreaming."

The Hairy Ape—naturalistic in its outlook, expressionistic in its method—was a turning point in O'Neill's playwrighting development. Wasting little pity on the hopeless primal horde, O'Neill next turned to the figure nearer his heart: the life-weary soul who could not belong, even to a world of apes, but who found the apes' prescription for survival—drinking and dope-

[4] *The Intimate Notebooks of George Jean Nathan* (New York, 1932), p. 180.
[5] *The Great God Brown*, Act I, scene 1.

dreaming—as effective as they had. O'Neill himself had long since been a confirmed inebriate. But alcohol was not entirely a refuge from reality; it also could heighten reality by stimulating the mystical faculties. It is "the great exciter," as William James observed, "of the *Yes* function in man."[6] O'Neill was a nay-sayer by temperament and habit, but he had a predilection for yea-saying and worked at it ardently so long as he was able. Since he was eighteen he had known the work of the most vociferous yea-sayer of them all and at last discovered a way to put Nietzsche to use.

In *The Birth of Tragedy* Nietzsche had perceived two forces operative in Greek tragedy before Euripides. The first of these he identified as Dionysian, its physiological analogue being the state of drunkenness. The other was the Apollonian, whose physiological analogue was dream. As a disciple of Nietzsche, O'Neill thus found a way to dignify his pathological tendencies. Nietzsche had a special appeal for O'Neill, as he had for scores of writers and countless readers in Europe and America during the first two decades of the twentieth century. Among the writers was Strindberg, whose temperament and genius were strikingly similar to Nietzsche's. It was the reading of Strindberg's plays when O'Neill first started to write in 1913, the Gelbs have reported him as saying, "that, above all else, first gave [him] the vision of what modern drama could be, and first inspired [him] with the urge to write for the theatre [himself]." Together, as the Gelbs have said, Nietzsche and Strindberg were O'Neill's literary heroes and "became in some ways a pattern for O'Neill's life."[7]

To those in the vanguard of American critics and writers Nietzsche offered a religion and an aesthetic, a mythology and a psychology. He provided a formula for such as O'Neill, who had repudiated both Scripture and Darwinism: substitute Dionysus for Christ, the satyr for the ape. He not only anticipated Freud; he helped clear the way for Freudianism. To the artist who wished to escape from realism he lent support by disparaging the "naturalistic and inartistic tendency." He offered the doctrine of Eternal Recurrence, his own version of death and rebirth. And to those, like O'Neill, who suffered from world-weariness and life-sickness, he taught struggle in place of resignation, ecstasy in place of denial. Such was the Dionysian way of life that O'Neill tried to adopt.

In his effort to resurrect Dionysus, O'Neill had the coopera-

[6]*The Varieties of Religious Experience* (New York, 1902), p. 378.
[7]Arthur and Barbara Gelb, *O'Neill* (New York, 1962), p. 234.

tion of his friends and associates Kenneth Macgowan and Robert Edmond Jones, who shared his apocalyptic fervor. The three of them took charge of the Provincetown Playhouse in 1923. In 1921 Macgowan had published a manifesto called *The Theater of To-morrow* that was a plea and a plan for the restoration of the theater to its original and proper function: a place for the "instinctive expression of godhead." "The problem," said Macgowan, "is to find a way for the religious spirit independent of the church," a way to make the theater itself religious. The drama, to achieve this end, must recognize man's identity with the "vast and unmanageable forces which have played through every atom of life since the beginning." Once he recovers his "sense of unity with the dumb, mysterious processes of nature,"[8] man once again will belong. Intoxicated by these grandiose conceptions, O'Neill set out to implement them.

He took tentative steps inside the theater of tomorrow when he converted his formula, dream and drunkenness, to vision and rapture, ending his plays in a high pitch of ecstatic affirmation. But not till *Desire under the Elms,* in 1924, did the Dionysian spirit manifest itself. It was at this time, too, that O'Neill began to dig at the roots of his own sickness. His father, mother, and brother had died between 1920 and the composition of *Desire under the Elms*. Imbued with Nietzschean defiance and vitality, he managed to overcome his grief, to affirm life, and to record its "most terrible and most questionable qualities," "declare them good and sanctify them."[9]—all as Nietzsche had directed. Thus O'Neill depicted in *Desire under the Elms* such assorted sins and crimes as greed, lechery, incest, adultery, revenge, and infanticide; he celebrated the triumph of pagan naturalism over indurated religion as well as the victory of mother and son over the father.

This was the first of many plays in which O'Neill presented the discordant unholy trinity of the father, the son, and the mother—the father usually menacing, the son at odds with him, the mother usually the protective and loving ally of the son. In *Desire under the Elms* Ephraim, the father, was the embodiment of harsh paternity, a religious fanatic, full of sexual prowess and physical strength (although he was seventy-five). He was invincible and indestructible, part Jehovah, part satyr. He was on good terms with all the creatures of his farm except his sons. His young wife, Abbie, was the personification of fecundity and of tender,

[8](New York, 1921), pp. 177, 264–65.
[9]*Beyond Good and Evil*, tr. Helen Zimmern (London, 1923), p. 228.

sinister maternity. Eben, the youngest son, was the victim of maternal deprivation and of the father, who scorned his weakness. By winning Abbie, the son triumphed at last over the father and gained a mother. Unrepentant, except for the crime of infanticide, son and mother-mistress paused, as they were being led off to jail at the end of the play, to kiss, to reaffirm their love, to admire the sunrise, to look up "raptly in attitudes aloof and devout."[10]

If Nietzsche stimulated O'Neill's imagination and helped him to release his inhibitions and write of deeply personal feelings, Freud and Jung illuminated the results. O'Neill knew the work of the analytic psychologists but, in perfect sincerity I think, denied their influence. His position was that of other writers before Freud became known outside his profession, writers of fiction and of drama who concerned themselves with the idea of father-son enmity, mother-son affection. Nevertheless, Freud's speculations on the origins of religion and morality in *Totem and Taboo* (1912, translated 1918) had an interesting relevance to the work of O'Neill. In that study Freud reconstructed the conditions of the primal horde, described a rebellion of the sons against the violent primal father who stood in the way of their sexual demands and of their desire for power. It was evident to Freud that, after the idea of God appeared, he was "in every case modelled after the father and that our personal relation to god is dependent upon our relation to our physical father, fluctuating and changing with him, and that god at bottom is nothing but an exalted father." The revolt was not of Satan but of the son, who was related to earlier conceptions of a god who had "enjoyed the favors of maternal deities and committed incest with the mother in defiance of the father,"[11] finally murdering the latter. In O'Neill's play if the old God—the father—is not yet dead, it is not because the son hadn't tried to kill him.

Eben's repeated plaintive appeal to his Maw was the earliest indication that O'Neill was to enlist the services of the mother in the struggle against the father and against God. In this he was a good, if unconscious, Jungian. For Jung, too, assigned the predominant role in the instinctual and spiritual world to the mother rather than to the father. The mother, he declared, "is the most immediate primordial image." The patient who "seeks to leave the world and to regain the subjectivity of childhood," the universal "secret longing for the maternal depths," "the childish longing for the food-giving mother,"[12] the marrying of a woman

[10](New York, 1925), Act III, scene 4.
[11](New York, 1938), pp. 919–20, 923.
[12]*Psychology of the Unconscious* (New York, 1949), p. 427.

who resembles the mother, personifications like Mother Earth, Mother Nature, Mother Church—these were all signs to Jung of the presence of a universal wish to enter the mother's womb a second time and be born again.

O'Neill continued under the aegis of Dionysus for two more plays, in the first of which, *The Great God Brown,* he had his heroes once again enjoy the ministrations of the mother. Abbie had been to all purposes an Earth Mother. She had given the son strength to defy God the Father, and now the Earth Mother, Cybel, helped him to fulfill the promise of the Gospels and to comfort his fear of death. Dion Anthony had been at odds not only with his father who, he mockingly said, "imagines he is God the Father," but with himself (out of desperation he had taken to drink), with God, with wife, and with sons. O'Neill began the play as though he intended to reveal the predicament of the American artist, stifled by a Philistine culture; but it became a personal allegory of the ordeal of the playwright himself. It became the lament of the shy, lonely, misunderstood young man, forsaken by his mother when she died and disappointed to find his wife an inadequate substitute. The mother, dominated by her "ogre" of a husband, was remembered by the son for her "purity." She was "stainless and imperishable." The wife, unfortunately, was "oblivious to everything but the means to her end of perpetuating the race" and therefore could offer neither understanding nor protection. The son had suffered his first great shock when he was four years old, after which he became an atheist. His playmate, he explained, had hit him with a stick, destroyed the picture he had drawn in the sand, and laughed when Dion cried. "I had loved and trusted him," said Dion, "and suddenly the good God was disproved in his person and the evil and injustice of Man was born!"[13] Longing to become a child again, Dion could not help but take a dim view of childhood.

Dion Anthony, in whom the "creative pagan acceptance of life" was at war with the masochistic, life-denying spirit of Christianity, became a tortured and torturing demonic ironist. Destitute of faith, he was terrified with skepticism. Longing for love—to be loved and protected—he was afraid to love. As death approached, Dion did become a child again. When his *alter ego,* William Brown, was dying, Brown was soothed by the Earth Mother, for he, too, was a sleepy child. A moment later he died, but only after he had experienced an ecstatic mystic insight concerning the Gospels: "Blessed are they that weep, for they shall

[13]Act II, scene 3.

laugh!" The child entered the kingdom of a heaven that resounds with laughter. The old God who was dead was replaced by a new one conceived in the image of Zarathustra the "godless," he who beseeched the "higher men" to learn how to laugh. As if such joy were not enough, O'Neill also invoked Nietzsche's doctrine of Eternal Recurrence, the "highest formula of affirmation that can ever be attained." "Always spring comes again bearing life!" the Earth Mother intoned. "Always again! . . . life again! summer and fall and death and peace again!"[14]

In *Lazarus Laughed* O'Neill ended his discipleship to Nietzsche, while making his last and most strenuous attempt to write for the Theater of Tomorrow. *Lazarus Laughed* was concerned with the rebirth of Dionysus, its theme being affirmation of life, denial of death. "The fear of death" O'Neill declared to be "the root of all evil." When Lazarus returned from death, his father was delighted to have him reborn to him. Thereafter, scene by scene, Lazarus became progressively younger, eventually to become a child and then to be born again without dying. Friction between father and son soon began when the former, whose God, like Ephraim Cabot's, was Jehovah, cursed the son for being of Jesus' party. When Jesus died, Jew and Christian alike displayed a vengeful fanaticism; and this was the occasion to replace both Jehovah and Christ with Lazarus, whom O'Neill then revealed to be Dionysus, whose prophet was Zarathustra. Zarathustra had preached his sermon, not on the mount but as he descended, exhorting Man, who was "once an ape" and who "remains more of an ape than any of the apes," to surpass himself, to become the Superman—a yea sayer and a laugher. "Laughing have I consecrated!" spake Zarathustra. "Ye higher men, learn, I pray you—to laugh!"[15] This was why Lazarus laughed. And yet he was Nietzsche's Dionysus with a difference. Although he was a yea sayer, a laugher, a lover of eternity, an exemplar of the doctrine of Eternal Recurrence, he was also loving, compassionate, maternal, and full of rapturous other-worldliness. Lazarus was, in short, the masculine counterpart of the Earth Mother and the pagan equivalent of Christ—the Mother and the Son in one person. O'Neill reconstructed everything to fill the heart's need: the conception of the Mother, the philosophy of Nietzsche, the teachings of Freud.

A spiritual epicurean, Lazarus rejected the egoistic belief in the immortality of the soul and argued that death was merely

[14]Act IV, scene 2.

[15]*Thus Spake Zarathustra*, tr. Thomas Common (Edinburgh, 1914), pp. 7, 363.

change, that Man must joyfully cooperate with the divine plan by willing his own annihilation. Having identified himself with the Universe, the Universe with himself, Man would belong and cease to be lonely. The tragedy was that he was unable to surpass himself, to accept the religion that Lazarus preached and for which he sacrificed himself. Appearing collectively as the Crowd, individually as Caligula (who squatted "monkey-wise" and referred to himself as "a trained ape"),[16] Man remained an ape— neither evil nor important, only despicable.

Although Lazarus was the embodiment of the most essential maternal attributes—comfort and love—he was not the only example of maternity in the play. Miriam, wife of Lazarus, was the counterpart of Dion Anthony's wife, who had been oblivious to everything but the means to her own end, a stubborn singleness of instinct that prevented her from understanding what her husband was getting at. Unable to comprehend that there is no death, Miriam persisted in weeping and mourning for the "dead." The other example of maternity was Livia, mother of Tiberius and the antithesis of Miriam. A sinister, "subtle, and crafty woman,"[17] she loved only power and used her son to gain that end. Deprived of tender, maternal love, Tiberius became the most contemptible of men. He not only hated others but loathed himself. Yet he, too, yearned for the innocence and love of early childhood, before he perceived that his mother had never loved him, before his great disillusionment.

After *Lazarus Laughed* O'Neill stopped writing plays for pagans. The rhapsodic quality left his work as the nay saying tendency returned, as the Bacchic reveler became once again the solitary drinker. The change coincided with, but was not caused by, the dissolution of the Macgowan-Jones-O'Neill triumvirate. O'Neill carried on with plays that were diminished in height but increased in length, plays in which he continued to diagnose the sickness of today without prescribing a Dionysiac—or, indeed, anything more than a sedative. *Strange Interlude* was a case in point. The play was about the heroine's life with father and, only incidentally, about life with husband, lover, and son, despite the fact that these relationships constituted the strange interlude that gave the piece its title. Nina Leeds's childhood relationship with her father was the single reality of her life. No Electra, she simply discovered that such love was enough, a love consisting of comfort, security, and peace. At the end of Act Nine, the interlude

[16]*Lazarus Laughed* (New York, 1927), Act II, scene I.
[17]Act IV, scene 1.

ended, she returned to her father's womblike lap, "warm in his love, safe-drifting into sleep."[18]

During the time of the interlude, extending from adolescence to menopause, Nina's experiences were mostly distressing. Here again the father played a significant part, for it had been his selfish meddling that prevented her marriage to a man who was soon to be killed in the war. Her feelings of guilt and of general unfulfillment precipitated the strange experiences that followed. "It was all your fault in the beginning, wasn't it?" Nina said to her father in Act Eight. "You mustn't ever meddle with human lives again." He had destroyed her happiness, made her self-conscious about her wickedness, caused her to punish herself, and had become for her a symbol of death. When she finally married Marsden, she was in effect marrying her father. In so doing she would be wedded to death, a consummation to be wished as devoutly as the above-mentioned childish benefits that she would also recover.

A neurotic, Nina was a portrait of the woman suffering from the sickness of today. As mother, wife, mistress, she combined attributes of Abbie, Cybel, and Livia; as daughter she was twin sister to Dion Anthony and a portrait of the artist as a young lady. She complained during the long interlude of many things, none of them tragic. Her passion spent, she declined into a gloomy pathos of self-pity. She discovered that happiness is ephemeral and therefore illusory; that words are merely sounds, appearances without realities; that the dead lover had been, after all, a mythical hero, the product of her romantic imagination; and that her search for God was unrewarding. Having rejected the "modern science God" for his indifference to her "misery of death-born-of-birth," she concluded that the mistake had begun "when God was created in a male image"—God the Father—"whose chest thunders with egotism and is too hard for tired heads and thoroughly comfortless."[19]

> We should have imagined life as created in the birthpain of God the Mother. Then we would understand why we, Her children, have inherited pain, for we would know that our life's rhythm beats from Her great heart, torn with the agony of love and birth. And we would feel that death meant reunion with Her, a passing back into Her substance, blood of Her blood again, peace of Her peace.[20]

[18](New York, 1928).
[19]Act II.
[20]*Ibid.*

Like Eben Cabot, the hero of *Dynamo*, the next play, longed for his dead mother. But this time an affair with another woman brought not peace but a tormenting sense of guilt. He pleaded "like a little boy": "I don't want to know the truth! I only want you to hide me, Mother! Never let me go from you again!"[21] Henceforth O'Neill was to find a meaning for guilt and sin. They were associated only with the Mother. On the other hand, so also were the supreme human needs, love and peace. Love was mother love, peace was in the womb. The theme of *Mourning Becomes Electra* was the yearning throughout death-in-life—a life perverted by the worship of God the Father—for what O'Neill called "death-birth-peace"[22]—the reward for worshipping God the Mother. At last he seemed to have found a new God who could satisfy his requirements. More than that, he contrived to write an approximation of Greek tragedy, which relied upon the concept of crime and retribution. Having passed beyond traditional good and evil he had then to reestablish a moral-religious system. This he did by basing it upon a matriarchy. If Freud could trace the beginning of religion and morality to the murder of the primordial father, O'Neill could seek their source in an offense against the primordial mother. Thus, the calamities that haunted the house of Mannon were traced to a central primal offense, the crime against Marie Brantôme, a mother, a crime whose classical counterpart was that which Atreus committed against his brother.

General Mannon—O'Neill's Agamemnon—had returned from war, seeking to love his wife and asking that she love him. Far from sacrificing a daughter, dallying at Appomattox, and bringing back a mistress, the General's only manifest crime had been the possession of a characteristic Mannon ineptitude where love was concerned. He was the personification of death-in-life, and his appearance was that of "a statue of an eminent dead man."[23] He was loved by no one, not even by his daughter Lavinia who, as Electra, should have behaved more Freudianly. Lavinia was the jealous rival of her mother, but not for the father's affections. She sought, rather, to depose the mother in order to succeed her, an aim that she achieved when her brother murdered the mother's lover, not to avenge his father's death (he had rejoiced in that) but in order to have the mother to himself. By

---

[21](New York, 1929), Act III, scene 3.

[22]"Working Notes and Extracts from a Fragmentary Work Diary," *New York Herald Tribune* (November 3, 1931).

[23]"The Hunted," Act III.

killing her lover he caused her death, after which he suffered the
deepest anguish of guilt. Cooperating with the Furies, Lavinia
suggested to him that he commit suicide. "Yes! That would be
justice," he said, "now you are Mother!" But then he realized
that "It's the way to peace—to find her again—my lost island—
Death is an Island of Peace, too—Mother will be waiting for me
there."[24] With the death of the brother, Lavinia was the last
Mannon. She broke the chain of crime and retribution by remaining unmarried and living with the dead inside the ancestral home.
"It takes the Mannons to punish themselves for being born," she
said, "with a strange cruel smile of gloating over the years of
self-torture"[25] that lay ahead. The great crime had been life itself;
living had been its retribution.

In *Lazarus Laughed* O'Neill had tried to deny death. In
Strange Interlude he had denied life but comforted his heroine
with recrudescent childishness. In *Mourning Becomes Electra* he
again denied life but let his heroine remain alive for the masochistic pleasure that it gave her. Having long since discharged
Dionysus, O'Neill next diminished the role of the Mother, paus-
ing first to write two plays: *Days without End,* in which he went
through the motions of returning to the faith that he had left as he
entered adolescence; and *Ah, Wilderness!* in which he recalled the summer of 1906, not as it was but as he wished it might
have been. Then in *The Iceman Cometh* he returned once again
to his past, to 1912. He was prepared to reduce the demands that
he had made of religion—love and peace—and that had been
supplied by the Mother. Peace alone now sufficed. To pay off the
curse of having been born, one punishes himself by remaining
alive. To the masochist that is a source of pleasure; but others, like
the derelicts in *The Iceman Cometh,* need to anesthetize themselves against the pain of living. Adrift between heaven and hell,
they were purgatorial ghosts silently punishing themselves without
suffering. For they had rediscovered the old family remedy—
drink and dope-dream—and found peace and contentment. But
the theme of the play was not how to live. O'Neill had developed
that theme in his early plays, when he had dealt with the life-
sustaining power of illusion. He was now discovering how to die.
Under the illusion that he was not afraid to die, the protagonist
waited for death, which could come only after he had surrendered
the last illusion. Peace would be his reward.

Whatever became of love? At one time O'Neill tried to speak
well of it. Thus, in an early play, he had converted sexual passion

[24]"The Haunted," Act III.
[25]*Ibid.,* Act IV.

into spiritual need and recorded the benefits of tender love between man and woman, recommending it as a way to conquer disease and death. One character had died of unrequited love. Another had claimed to love love. Still another hated men but loved Man. Then love came to be associated exclusively with the mother, love in its purest, most durable form. At last it occurred to one of the later heroes that perhaps in his soul he hated love. And now in *The Iceman Cometh* O'Neill demonstrated not only that truth, justice, and faith are illusory but that love is nonexistent, that it is a pipedream. The main business of the play was to unmask love—all forms, including that of the Mother. A destructive pipe dream, love generated shame, guilt, hate, and death.

O'Neill had long been aware of the face behind the mask, of reality behind appearance, but he had never before given more than a furtive glance at the "skull beneath the skin." "Much possessed by death,"[26] he had written *Lazarus Laughed,* in which he tried to deny its existence; *Strange Interlude,* in which the heroine's fleeting fear of death was comforted by returning to the peace, protection, and comfort of childhood; and *Mourning Becomes Electra,* in which the son saw death as a return to the Mother and in which the daughter thought of it as a kind of dessert. *The Iceman Cometh* put an end to evasion. O'Neill faced his death at last. Having come to terms with it, he was prepared next to "face his dead,"[27] as he put it, and to come to terms with them. They had haunted his plays for the past twenty years. In *Long Day's Journey into Night* he shut himself in with the O'Neill dead, as Lavinia had with the Mannon dead, to display the family skeletons. O'Neill went back to 1912 once more, to show his father as he really was—not God the Father, not an ogre, not the statue of an eminent dead man, but a credible, picturesque, pitiful human being—and the mother—not God the Mother, not loving and protective, but romantically self-deceived, wistful, weak, childlike, even sinister in her vengefulness and in her efforts to vindicate herself. As she set out early in the morning on her "long day's journey into night," a ghost-like figure slowly disappearing into the fog of morphine addiction, of dope-dream and oblivion, father and sons, filled with dismay, disgust, and guilt, looked on helplessly, comforted only by whisky. "It's as if, in spite of loving us, she hated us!" said Edmund-Eugene. It seemed to him that she took morphine only for its effect, deliberately to create "a bank of fog in which she

[26]T. S. Eliot, "Whispers of Immortality," *Collected Poems* (New York, 1936), p. 61.
[27]*Long Day's Journey into Night* (New Haven, 1956), Dedication.

hides and loses herself . . . to get beyond our reach, to be rid of
us, to forget we're alive!"[28] The fog was a symbol of peace, a
refuge for those who must escape not only from life but from love.
Jamie, the dissolute brother, also mystified O'Neill. The infer-
ence was that he drank for the same reason that the mother took
narcotics: the defect of love. This was the rock upon which the
family had foundered.

During all those years O'Neill had been reliving his adolescent experiences and agonies and had failed to come so close to
diagnosing the sickness. His heroes, however much they spoke of
loving and strove to love, never convincingly succeeded. For in
their childish self-obsession they demanded love only for themselves. Aware of this, O'Neill repudiated it entirely in *The Iceman Cometh*. Then, the following year, in *Long Day's Journey*,
he reversed himself, risking the loss of peace for the sake of
love—or if not quite love, then its close equivalent: "pity and
understanding and forgiveness."[29] He tried to absolve not only
himself but his family as well. O'Neill culminated both his quest
and his career with *Long Day's Journey* and *The Iceman Cometh*. I am convinced that they are not only his finest plays but that
they have not been surpassed anywhere since they were written.

He wrote one more play, his very last, and a comparatively
feeble one, *A Moon for the Misbegotten*—about the older
brother. Approaching the end of his life in 1923, Jamie was tormented with guilt over his feelings about the recently dead
mother. Through the love of Josie, an oversize, powerful young
woman, he was made at last to feel "at peace with [himself] and
this lousy life—as if all [his] sins had been forgiven." Josie started
out as if she were going to be the counterpart of Abbie in *Desire
under the Elms*, but O'Neill made a special point later in the play
of her virginity. She was not only a virgin Earth Mother, she was
the Virgin herself, "this big sorrowful woman hugging a haggard-
faced, middle-aged drunkard against her breast, as if he were a
sick child."[30] The image that O'Neill evoked was that of the
Virgin and Child, the *Pietà*, or a combination of the two—a tableau grotesque but not blasphemous. Once again he had come as
close to love and pity as he ever had. To be sure, he saw in his
brother Jamie his own character and his own plight. That was a
reality that at this stage of his career he would not have denied or
evaded. If self-love and self-pity were the face behind the mask of
love, so be it.

Tormented though he himself was, O'Neill was spared his brother's fate, and that of his sons. His playwriting must have saved him. The theater, which he had once tried to make religious, was a substitute for the Church which he had left and served him probably as the Church would have, as a place of refuge rather than of worship. As a poet he tried to "transmute his personal and private agonies into something rich and strange, something universal and impersonal."[31] But succeeding or failing, he used the theater as a vast public confessional, a great therapeutic couch. To be sure, he could not have done that were it not for his impressive talent, his technical skill, his knowledge of the theater. Were it not for that, he, too, would probably have been a derelict or a suicide like the other male members of his family—with the exception of his gifted father.

O'Neill examined his "sickness of today" with monomaniacal concentration and intensity, repeatedly tracing it to the source of infection. This backward tendency was apparent even in the naturalistic early plays. And he himself was conscious of it. One of his characters called it "the cowardly yearning to go back,"[32] but back he always went. Whether to cheer himself up or to exercise the artist's prerogative, he transformed family, religion, philosophy, psychology, and pathology (alcoholism, neurotic fixation, inordinate fear of death, terror of skepticism) to fit his personal and dramatic requirements. His intensity of feeling too often had no objective equivalent in the plays. When he strained to communicate what was repressed or what was ineffable, he was often awkward, banal, and prolix. His ambition to do big work in the theater—to surpass his father, some critics think—resulted frequently in something grandiose, turgid, adolescent, even ludicrous. Many of the foregoing features were obscured in production, for O'Neill's drama played better than it read, as drama should. But it was not only staging that rescued the plays, nor was it their novelty—experiments with the masks, the asides, and so forth; it was something organic, the product of O'Neill's dramatic imagination and sense of artistic form. I am referring to what O'Neill called the "mystical pattern which manifests itself as an overtone"[33] and which, when it was permitted to do its own work, enriched the play and communicated idea and emotion more effectively than did the language of the piece. The organic presence of symbol and myth—Biblical, pagan,

---

[31]T. S. Eliot, "Shakespeare and the Stoicism of Seneca," *Selected Essays* (New York, 1932), p. 117.

[32]*Days without End*, Act 1.

[33]The New York *Evening Post* (February 13, 1926).

psychological—was one of the very impressive aspects of O'Neill's playwriting. It was best exemplified, I think, by *Desire under the Elms;* but it was effective, too, in *Strange Interlude, Mourning Becomes Electra, The Iceman Cometh* (in which Cyrus Day has discerned interesting Biblical resemblances), and in the Epiphany-like scene of *A Moon for the Misbegotten.* I am referring also to the structure of the plays, a case in point being *Long Day's Journey into Night,* which Eric Bentley has described as

> a kind of classical quartet. Here O'Neill eschews the luxury of numerous minor characters, crowds, and a bustle of stage activity. He has a few people and they talk. This has given the public an impression of shapelessness. . . . *Long Day's Journey* is a dramatic achievement which at first glance *seems* formless. Later, one discovers the form. The play has the outward calm and formality— not formlessness!—of French classical tragedies. Like them—and like *The Iceman*—it observes the unities.[34]

In the many plays in which O'Neill did not observe the neoclassical unities he achieved form through the cyclic arrangement of the action: the identity of the end and the beginning, the eternal return, the backward tendency. Form and idea were one. And so, too, were art and life. When O'Neill lay dying, he is said to have "clenched his fists, raised himself . . . in his bed and gasped: 'Born in a hotel room—and God damn it—died in a hotel room!' "[35]—a most appropriate epitaph.

[34]"Eugene O'Neill," in *Major Writers of America,* ed. Perry Miller (New York, 1962), II, 570.

[35]Arthur and Barbara Gelb, *O'Neill,* p. 939.

Frederic I. Carpenter

Eugene O'Neill, the Orient, and American Transcendentalism

In this essay I shall not attempt to define Eugene O'Neill's "transcendentalism." Instead, I shall trace his attitude toward the historic American Transcendentalists, especially Thoreau. And I shall relate this to his life-long interest in the Orient—an interest which he shared with the earlier Transcendentalists. In one sense O'Neill was more of an Orientalist than Emerson or Thoreau had ever been.

I

Toward the American Transcendentalists, O'Neill's feelings were often ambivalent. The mixture of admiration and irony with which he regarded them suggests one of the many paradoxes of his nature. Whether he reacted as a member of the younger generation toward the literary tastes of his father, or as the son of an Irish immigrant toward the social idealism of an earlier New England, his feelings were mixed. The Transcendentalists had been rebels against the materialism of their times, but their idealism had also been the product of a Yankee and Puritan society.

In the New London house of James O'Neill, Sr., Emerson's books had been available on the library shelves, and the young Eugene probably read them there.[1] He later put some of the mysticism of Emerson's "Brahma" into the mouth of his own Lazarus, who proclaimed: "We are the Giver and the Gift!" But it is probable that he derived most of this "transcendentalism" from his favorite author, Nietzsche, whose "Zarathustra" had earlier been inspired by Emerson.

[1]Arthur and Barbara Gelb, *O'Neill* (New York, 1962), pp. 84, 88.

From Transcendentalism and its Legacy, *edited by Myron Simon and Thornton H. Parsons. Copyright © 1966 by the University of Michigan. Reprinted by permission of the University of Michigan Press.*

More ironically, O'Neill remembered the older Transcendentalism when he bought a country house at Ridgefield, Connecticut, named "Brook Farm," and composed there his famous *Desire under the Elms*. The contrast of the naturalism of the modern play with the earlier idealism seems obvious; yet, more subtly, this modern *Desire* also translated the earlier irony suggested by the "Spirit of Nature" in Emerson's "Hamatreya": " 'Mine, not yours. / Earth endures.' " Both in the play and in the earlier poem, the true hero is Nature, who brings tragedy equally to the desires of the Cabots, and to the possessiveness of "Bulkeley, Hunt, Willard, Hosmer, Meriam, Flint."

As O'Neill grew older, his theme of possessiveness seemed to become increasingly obsessive, and gradually the idea of a cycle of plays about American history developed in his mind. The title should be: "A Tale of Possessors Self-Dispossessed." And the ironic contrast between his later pessimism and his earlier idealism was sharpened by the borrowing of a title from Oliver Wendell Holmes' "The Chambered Nautilus"—"Build thee more stately mansions, O my soul." Emphasizing only the materialistic drive of modern American civilization, O'Neill now sought to dramatize its continuing struggle to build "More Stately Mansions."

This contrast between an earlier idealism and a later pessimism is emphasized even more sharply by O'Neill's changing attitudes toward Thoreau. In *Lazarus Laughed* he had made his hero paraphrase Thoreau, in replying to the question: "What did you find beyond there, Lazarus?" Replying to a similar question on his death-bed, Thoreau is reported to have said: "One world at a time." Now Lazarus replies. "Is not one world in which you know not how to live enough for you?"

But after dramatizing the mystical idealism of Lazarus in transcendental terms, O'Neill seems to have become increasingly skeptical of the practical aspects of Thoreau's Transcendentalism. And when he began work on his ambitious new "Cycle," which, he hoped, would progressively dramatize "the story of America," he imagined a strikingly Thoreauvian character as the founder of his projected "Irish-American family." But he imagined Simon Harford, the Thoreauvian hermit, as a disillusioned idealist, in process of abandoning his romantic and poetic dreams of "living the simple life" beside his pond. And now Simon's unillusioned mother, Deborah Harford, observes ironically to her future Irish daughter-in-law, Sara Melody, that: "evidently he has found a new romantic dream by way of recompense." *A*

Touch of the Poet centers upon the hero's abandonment of his earlier "transcendental dream," for a "new romantic dream," which gradually turns into the wholly "material dream" of amassing a fortune and building "more stately mansions."

That Simon Harford, the "hero" of *A Touch of the Poet* and of *More Stately Mansions*, was partly modeled after the historic Thoreau, seems self-evident. But a recent article by Professor Mordecai Marcus[2] has argued that Deborah Harford, his mother, was also suggested by Thoreau's mother (who was not always too happy about her son's Transcendental individualism), and that Cornelius Melody, the Irish father-in-law, was himself suggested by an Irish tavern-keeper described vividly in Thoreau's *Journal*—a romantic but disreputable character who had known better days. O'Neill had pretty certainly been reading Thoreau's *Journal* while planning his famous "Cycle." But the remarkable fact is that he should have changed the character of his Thoreauvian hermit so radically. For the historic Thoreau, of course, had never been seduced by any conventionally romantic enganglement, and had never capitulated to American "materialism."

An explanation of O'Neill's distortion of the character of his hermit in *A Touch of the Poet* is suggested by Deborah Harford's repeated use of the word "dream" to describe her son's deluded idealism. His dream, like his father's and his grandfather's before him, was "fanatic" and Byronic. "I cannot imagine you taking that seriously," Deborah exclaims. Therefore, because it was wholly illusory, it soon became a "romantic dream," and then a "material dream." In an interview reported by Hamilton Basso about this time, O'Neill explained: "We talk about the American Dream, and want to tell the world about the American Dream, but what is that dream, in most cases, but the dream of material things? I sometimes think that the United States, for this reason, is the greatest failure the world has ever seen."[3] In other words, O'Neill believed that Thoreau's American Dream had been essentially a "pipe dream," like the delusions of the denizens of Harry Hope's saloon in *The Iceman Cometh*. It was a delusion whose failure inevitably led to "the dream of material things."

To O'Neill's mind, therefore, the failure of Thoreau's dream of "saving our souls by being content with little," led inevitably toward the symbolic disillusion of "Hope" in *The Iceman*. His-

---

[2]Mordecai Marcus, "Eugene O'Neill's Debt to Thoreau in *A Touch of the Poet*," *JEGP*, LXII (April 1963), 270–79.

[3]Hamilton Basso, "The Tragic Sense," *The New Yorker*, XXIV (March 13, 1948), 37–40.

torically, Emerson, Thoreau, and the Transcendentalists had all imaged the future realization of "the American Dream" in history. But now O'Neill dramatized the later disillusion of "the modern temper." And it seems that his later pessimism expressed his own progressive disillusion.

Nevertheless, it can be argued that O'Neill's denial of "Hope," and his rejection of Thoreau's "American Dream," should not be interpreted merely as "disillusion." His modern pessimism gave expression to another aspect of the historic Transcendental philosophy, and even suggested echoes of Emerson's own "Illusions." O'Neill's emphasis on the necessary defeat of all human illusions merely repeated the ancient Oriental philosophy which Emerson and Thoreau had also shared. But where the historic Transcendentalists had interpreted Oriental idealism in terms of pragmatic action, O'Neill rejected their pragmatism in favor of an older quietism. His disagreement with the American Transcendentalists lay in his total rejection of the American philosophy of pragmatism, and in his acceptance of a purer Orientalism.

II

O'Neill's Orientalism is—I think—the most important and distinctive aspect of his art, and yet the most difficult to define. I have tried to suggest its effect upon his dramas in a recent book.[4] This essay will describe the more specific evidences of his interest in the Orient and its philosphy.

From the beginning his dramas expressed a compelling—if often vague—fascination with the Orient. The hero of his first full-length play to be produced—Andrew Mayo in *Beyond the Horizon*—emphatically proclaimed his idealization of "the beauty of the far off and unknown, the mystery and spell of the East which lures me in the books I've read." And the later hero of *The Fountain,* Ponce de Leon, also described his mythical quest for "some far country of the East—Cathay, Cipango, who knows—a spot that Nature has set apart from men and blessed with peace."

At the height of his career, however, O'Neill wrote two dramas to describe more fully the meeting of East and West. And both used Eastern philosophy to comment upon the materialism

[4]Frederic I. Carpenter, *Eugene O'Neill* (New York, 1964).

of the West. In *Marco Millions* the hero travels through Persia and India to confront "the Great Kaan" of China. Then, after Marco has made his "millions" and departed, leaving tragedy behind him, the priests of the four great religions of the East seek to console the Great Kaan. Buddhism, Taoism, Confucianism, and Islam offer their wisdom in turn. But the medieval "Babbitt" from the West has proved too much for them.

Following *Marco Millions,* O'Neill wrote his most ambitious—and most imaginative—drama of ideas. In *Lazarus Laughed* he dramatized what he believed the essential message of all religions. His ideal Lazarus strove to realize the gospel of the resurrected Christ, and, in the second scene, visited Greece to suggest the similarity of his gospel to that of the Greek god Dionysus. But then, more subtly, he went on to identify his message with that of the religions of the Orient. In the third act, the Emperor Tiberius has crucified an Asiatic lion, adding the scornful comment: "From the East, land of false gods and superstition, this lion was brought to Rome to amuse Caesar." Now Lazarus befriends the lion, which licks his hand as a sign of sympathy. In an article on *"Lazarus Laughed* and Buddha"[5] Doris Alexander has shown that this action repeats a pattern common to Buddhist legend, and has suggested many parallels between the story of Lazarus and the legends and teachings of Buddhism.

In *Lazarus Laughed,* indeed, O'Neill may be said to have defined his Orientalism in terms of dramatic action. Because he explicitly compared his Lazarus to the Greek Dionysus, and because he always avowed his enthusiasm for Nietzsche's *Thus Spake Zarathustra* and *The Birth of Tragedy,* Lazarus has sometimes been said to preach the Nietzschean gospel of the superman. Yet O'Neill's Lazarus was no Occidental superman, performing victorious acts of the will. Rather, he became an Oriental superman, whose triumph was that he refused to act in opposition to evil. And his greatest triumph came when he refused to act to prevent the death of his wife, Miriam, at the hands of the Romans. His final victory was an inner victory over his own selfish attachment to life.

Not only *Marco Millions* and *Lazarus Laughed,* but all of O'Neill's dramas of this period show evidences of his interest in Oriental ideas. *The Great God Brown,* for instance, described Cybel with humorous incongruity: "She chews gum like a sacred cow forgetting time with an eternal end." And Dion Anthony

[5]Doris M. Alexander, *"Lazarus Laughed* and Buddha," *Modern Language Quarterly,* XVII (Dec. 1956), 357–65.

remarked: "One must do something to pass away the time while one is waiting—for one's next incarnation." Similarly, the giant "Dynamo," which gives its name to the following play, is described as having "oil switches . . . their six cupped arms stretching upward . . . like queer Hindu idols tortured into scientific supplications."

In 1930, after having studied Emerson's reading and interpretation of Oriental ideas, I called attention to O'Neill's apparent Orientalism in the last chapter of a book on *Emerson and Asia*. And in 1932 I wrote to ask information of O'Neill. On June 24, 1932, he replied from Sea Island, Georgia:

> As for your question regarding Oriental ideas, I do not think they have influenced my plays at all. Certainly, not consciously. Many years ago I did considerable reading in Oriental philosophy and religion, however, although I never went in for an intensive study of it. I simply did it in order to have some sort of grasp of the subject as part of my philosophical background. The mysticism of Lao-tse and Chuang-Tzu probably interested me more than any other Oriental writing.[6]

O'Neill's emphatic disclaimer, asserting flatly that "I do not think Oriental ideas have influenced my plays at all," obviously must be discounted. Not only do his later remarks in this letter qualify it, but similar disclaimers of his suggest that he tended to minimize any "influences" from other authors or ideas, in order to assert his own creative originality. In discussing his debt to Freud and Jung, for instance, he made a similar disclaimer in a letter to Martha Sparrow.[7] Nevertheless, is is probable that he read Oriental literature less intensively—and less extensively— than might be supposed.

The original source of O'Neill's Orientalism has recently been discovered by Doris Alexander.[8] And this source was not so much literary as personal. A close friend of O'Neill's early days at "The Hell Hole" was Terry Carlin, an alcoholic philosopher who loved to discourse on the wisdom of the Orient to all who would listen. A worshiper of Dionysus both in practice and in theory, he also introduced the young O'Neill to a book of mystical theosophy entitled *Light on the Path*. And from this

[6]From a holograph letter to F. I. Carpenter. Quoted by permission.

[7]Quoted in an article by Arthur H. Nethercot, "The Psychoanalyzing of Eugene O'Neill," *Modern Drama*, III (Dec. 1960), 242–56.

[8]Doris M. Alexander, "Eugene O'Neill and *Light on the Path*," *Modern Drama*, III (Dec. 1960), 260–67.

subliterary book, proclaimed by this hobo philosopher, O'Neill first learned of the Orient and its ideas.

Later, in 1928, after writing *Lazarus Laughed* and *Marco Millions,* O'Neill left America on a voyage to the Orient. In the actual Orient, however, he found only disillusion with the desperate poverty and squalor which he saw; and in Shanghai he went on one last, desperate, alcoholic binge, which ended in a hospital. Cathay, the country of his early dreams, apparently destroyed his last illusions.

And yet, eight years later, when the O'Neills moved to California and built a new house there, they named it "Tao House." And the name invoked again the old mystical religion of Lao-tse, which he had read more than a decade before. Certain features of the house and grounds suggested Chinese ideas and superstititions: the garden paths, for instance, were laid in zig-zags, remembering an old Chinese superstition that evil spirits could only travel in straight lines. And yet there is no evidence to support the assertion of Croswell Bowen that "Eugene O'Neill, like so many people who settle in the San Francisco area, quite suddenly took up Oriental philosophy."[9] Rather the opposite. The name of "Tao House" merely reaffirmed O'Neill's old fascination with Oriental ideas. Even his disillusion with the actual Orient could not destroy his life-long faith in Oriental mysticism.

III

The facts of O'Neill's lifelong interest in the Orient point toward some important conclusions. His Orientalism was much less literary than was Emerson's. It was more personal in origin, and more temperamental in expression. Moreover, it was much less concerned with facts and with actions, and it was more concerned with internal feelings and attitudes. But for this very reason, O'Neill's Orientalism seems more genuinely "Oriental" than Emerson's. For the Orient has always been less concerned with facts, and more concerned with internal feelings, than has the Occident.

O'Neill's lack of concern with the external realities of science and social action, and, indeed, his very hostility toward "material things," seems to set him apart from the mainstream of American literature and thought. It also helps to explain his differences with the historic American Transcendentalists. Al-

[9]Croswell Bowen. *The Curse of the Misbegotten* (New York, 1959), p. 259.

though Emerson and Thoreau believed that "Things are in the saddle, / And ride mankind," they never scorned material things. Rather, they sought to ameliorate the actual situation, and they appealed to the future. But O'Neill disbelieved in the future, and in "Hope." He considered tragedy to be essential to the nature of things. Yet this belief made him, in a sense, even more "transcendental" than Emerson.

Historic Transcendentalism has, in fact, divided into two streams. The first has become active, scientific, and pragmatic. The second has become passive, mystical, and psychological. Emerson's thought flowed largely in the first stream, toward modern pragmatism. O'Neill's thought tended towards modern, nonrational psychology.

Early in his career, O'Neill had explained the general principles which were to guide his whole theory and practice of playwriting. "Our emotions are a better guide than our thoughts," he asserted in 1922. "Our emotions are instinctive. They are the result not only of our individual experiences but of the experiences of the whole human race, back through all the ages."[10] Like modern depth psychology, O'Neill's dramas always probed man's emotions, rather than his thoughts and actions.

Yet, in a sense, both O'Neill's dramas and modern depth psychology were melioristic, and "hopeful." In another statement made in 1922, O'Neill explained: "It seems to me that . . . man is much the same creature, with the same primal emotions and ambitions and motives, the same powers and the same weaknesses, as in the time when the Aryan race started toward Europe from the slopes of the Himalayas. He has become better acquainted with those powers and those weaknesses, and he is learning ever so slowly how to control them."[11] O'Neill's tragic dramas were directed toward the understanding of man's "primal emotions," rather than his pragmatic actions. This goal resembled that of the Oriental religion which originated on "the slopes of the Himalayas." Thus, O'Neill clung to one, last, melioristic illusion. He hoped that man, by means of the insight into human emotions suggested by tragic drama, might ultimately learn to "know himself," and through knowledge, "ever so slowly," control.

[10]Mary B. Mullett, "The Extraordinary Story of Eugene O'Neill," *American Magazine,* XCIV (Nov. 1922), 34, 112–20.
[11]Oliver M. Sayler, "The Real Eugene O'Neill," *The Century Magazine,* CIII (Jan. 1922), 351–59.

Peter J. Gillett

O'Neill and the Racial Myths

Until about 1940, various crushing handicaps prevented black authors from presenting the black experience cogently to a suitable public, and so the task of creating developed and truly representative black characters in works of sufficient literary merit to compel an audience fell chiefly upon white writers. Among the distinguished whites who accepted the challenge were Melville, Mark Twain, Conrad, Faulkner, and Eugene O'Neill. The challenge was a severe one for them partly because their own experience was perforce very remote from the black experience—color being a far greater barrier than, say, sex or social class—and partly because of a fact just as galling to black writers, that in America and Europe a black character cannot serve as vehicle for a universal theme: Everyman, in the West, is a white man. But their greatest difficulty, probably, lay in a set of received "truths" about black people, notions which we nowadays include among the racial myths but which, we must remember, were hard to transcend since blacks as well as whites at least partially accepted them.

In his response to this challenge O'Neill may perhaps be the most interesting of all white authors. It would have been quite understandable in the circumstances had he uncritically incorporated the racial myths in his work. For in the period spanned by his five so-called "negro plays," from 1914 to 1924, anthropology and psychology tended to give weight to some of the myths; moreover the last two of these five, *The Emperor Jones* and *All God's Chillun Got Wings,* coincided with the early days of the "Harlem Renaissance," in which black writers themselves often treated the black man as a primitive. Despite this—and herein, I believe, lies the interest of his treatment of the black American—in these five plays and in *The Iceman Cometh* (1946) O'Neill met the various difficulties of presenting black characters with ever greater assurance, awareness, and success. As we move from

From Twentieth Century Literature, *XVIII (January–October 1972). Reprinted by permission.*

Thirst through *The Iceman* we can watch America's most influential playwright more and more understanding blackness as part of the black man's humanity, and in the process sloughing off the influence of the traditional American racial myths.

The remarks of some critics on *All God's Chillun* might, however, lead one to believe almost the opposite, and before examining all the plays in turn we would do well to look at this one rather closely, scrutinizing especially its controversial ending. Jim Harris, its black protagonist, is repeatedly foiled in his ambition to succeed in the white profession of the law by his feeling of inferiority to the white world. This feeling becomes explicit on several occasions, but especially when he proposes to the white girl, Ella, with whom he fell in love in his early teens. "I don't want nothing," he protests in romantic ardor, "—only . . . to serve you—. . . to preserve and protect and shield you . . . to become your slave!—yes, be your slave—your black slave that adores you as sacred!" The passage, as has been recognized, is an adaptation of Adler's psychological theory, according to which frustration of the innate "will to power" produced neurosis which might show itself in self-submission and self-humiliation; it also embodies the contemporary notion that a man's behavior was conditioned by his racial heritage;[1] it is also, much more importantly, an instance of O'Neill's talent for transmuting the abstractions of psychology into vital characters and significant art. It beautifully merges the hard fact of black slavery with a sentimental stock metaphor of romantic love to produce a disturbing and resonant ambiguity; and it foreshadows, and helps explain, the ending.

Two years after their marriage, Jim and Ella return from France disillusioned. They have failed to drown their difference of color, and the conflict between Ella's conscious love for Jim's humanity and her unconscious hatred of his blackness is driving her into insanity and into enmity with his academically successful sister, Hattie. At one moment she encourages Jim in his studies, at the next she is a little child who wants only to play games with "old Uncle Jim who's been with us for years and years," at the next a homicidal monster with a carving knife, screaming "You dirty nigger!" at her husband. In the last scene she finds the source of all their miseries in the grotesque Congo mask hanging on the parlor wall: "It's you who're to blame for this! But why'd you want to do this to us? . . . I married you, didn't I? Why don't

[1] Edwin A. Engel, *The Haunted Heroes of Eugene O'Neill* (Cambridge, Mass., 1953), pp. 117–20.

you let Jim alone? . . . He's white, isn't he—the whitest man that ever lived? Why do you come in to interfere? Black! Black! Black is dirt!" When Jim returns with the news of his latest failure in the law examinations, she openly rejoices, apparently thinking he ought to rejoice too. In her joy she "grabs the mask from its place, sets it in the middle of the table and plunging the knife down through it pins it to the table." She has killed her devil, she thinks. But as the Emperor Jones can only kill his devil by virtually killing himself, as the boys in *Lord of the Flies* have to kill "the Beast" over and over and still live in terror of it, so Ella's devil still lives. After a moment of rage in which he calls her a "white devil woman," Jim subsides. He will never aspire again. His metaphor of slavery has become truth. As Ella says, "brightly," "Well, it's all over now."

The ending which follows, in its bitter, ironic, twentieth-century way, is masterly. Some critics, indeed, have seen in Jim's self-abasement a mere escape. According to one, he "lacks not only the courage to face his problems, and the heroism to fight against them, but also the self-knowledge to understand them. . . . The spiritual 'wings' which 'exalt' Jim Harris are not those of tragic understanding and self-transcendence; they are those of pathetic defeat and self-delusion."[2] Another calls the last scene an anti-climax, which evades the tragedy of Jim and Ella by letting them revert to childishness while representing Jim's closing words as an enlightenment.[3] But T. S. Eliot, in his brief review, was right: "Mr. O'Neill has got hold of a 'strong plot'; he not only understands one aspect of the 'negro problem,' but he succeeds in giving this problem universality in implying . . . the universal problem of differences which create a mixture of admiration, love, and contempt, with the consequent tension. . . . The close is magnificent."[4]

From the moment when Jim cuts short his talk of how and why we wanted to become a lawyer—the moment, presumably, when he realizes that the time for futile aspiration is over and the time for something new has come—from this moment Ella, "chat-

[2]Frederic I. Carpenter, *Eugene O'Neill* (Twayne Series, New York, 1964), p. 104.

[3]Francis Fergusson, "Eugene O'Neill," *Hound and Horn* (Jan., 1930), repr. under the title "Melodramatist" in Oscar Cargill, N. Bryllion Fagin, and William J. Fisher, eds., *O'Neill and His Plays: Four Decades of Criticism* (New York 1961), p. 275.

[4]*New Criterion* 4 (Apr., 1926), 395–96, repr. in Cargill *et al.,* p. 169. Eliot's words on "universality" chime quite well with O'Neill's own, quoted by Arthur and Barbara Gelb, *O'Neill* (New York 1960), pp. 535–36. Engel (pp. 121–26) is with the angels too.

tering along," sketches out their future. Sometimes they will play
at being the little boy and girl who fell in love in Act I Scene i.
Sometimes, in a kind of racial transvestism, she will black her face
while he chalks his—in the first scene Jim envied "Painty Face's"
complexion, and she wished she were black. Sometimes he will be
her "old kind Uncle Jim who's been with us for years and years."
And he must "never, never, never, never" leave her. With utter
ingenuousness, she speaks of her total dependence on him, her
love for him. And suddenly, with "shining eyes" and "transfi-
gured face," Jim drops to his knees and prays, beginning as he
prays to "weep in an ecstasy of religious humility." "Let this fire
of burning suffering," he begs God, "purify me of selfishness and
make me worthy of the child You send me for the woman You
took away!" This approaches the very brink of maudlin
religiosity—the two are as close, and as polar, as are "Hearts and
Flowers" and the slow movement of Beethoven's Ninth, or far-
left and far-right politics.

   To understand this remarkable ending at all, we must see the
whole play in two ways at once—both as a story of love and
marriage perverted by destiny, by an ineradicable and ever-
visible difference between the protagonists, and as an image of
relations between the races in America. It is, beyond dispute,
both of these, yet reviewers and critics have often chosen to look
upon it as only one or the other. Much of the criticism is vague to
the point of meaninglessness, perhaps because of the well-
intentioned urge of liberal whites to get rid of the "negro problem" by simply not seeing it. In Act I Scene ii Joe taunts Jim with
his white aspirations: "What's all dis schoolin' you doin'? What's
all dis dressin' up and graduatin' and sayin' you gwine study be a
lawyer? . . . What's all dis denyin' you's a nigger . . .? Is you
aimin' to buy white wid yo' ol' man's dough . . .? What is
you? . . . Is you a nigger or isn't you? Is you a nigger, Nigger?
Nigger, is you a nigger?" And Jim replies, quietly, deflating Joe's
rage, "Yes. I'm a nigger. We're both niggers." Eliot, of course,
was right in saying that the play points through and beyond the
question of race to all those differences which thwart and pervert
human affections; but a critic who can see in such dialogue *only* a
universal drama of souls, or who can see the play *only* as a drama
of marriage, is surely both white and half-blind. The inevitable
result of such one-eyed views is the complaint that Act I Scene i
is unnecessary for the play's thematic development while the last
scene is a melodramatic and bathetic evasion.[5] Such criticism

[5]Fergusson (Cargill *et al.*, pp. 274–75).

assumes that the theme is the conflict between a man's work and his wife, or love thwarted by social ostracism, and makes this assumption in defiance not only of the first scene but of the presence of Hattie, the stark black-and-white symbolism of Act I Scene iv, and many other features of the play. If O'Neill had desired to use the difference of race merely as motivation for a story of marriage, he, with his theatrical experience and his expressionistic proclivity, would certainly have realized that all other indications of the difference were rendered superfluous by the mere color of the actors' faces.

Looking at the play as a story of a crippled marriage, and suspending for a time our judgment as to the relevance of, for instance, the opening scene, we see that in the moment after Ella has stabbed the mask Jim has three, or perhaps four, choices. He can break up the marriage by divorcing Ella or committing her to an asylum, as Hattie advised. This course might have enabled him to contribute, like Hattie, to the liberation of his people; but probably, in view of his performance in examinations before he married Ella, he would have failed again—and while, of course, no one could justly blame him for breaking his bondage to a schizophrenic and dangerous woman, the course he actually takes is nobler. He can, alternatively, kill her—a finely symbolic action, but a poor way to reconcile the claims to happiness of two people tied to each other. He can choose to live like Mr. Rochester with an imprisoned Gothic madwoman. Or he can do what he does.

A marriage—to perpetrate a platitude—is a compromise between two creatures who, being human, are unique. If the partners can, nevertheless, find happiness in conventionally approved ways, the marriage has a good chance of succeeding. But if just one of them is incurably "different" in mentality, incurably unconventional (the word "perverted" is unsuitably loaded for this context)—if, in other words, one of them can only find happiness in some way of which society disapproves, then either the marriage must end in separation, divorce, even murder, or the other partner must deliberately and radically change himself so as to find his own happiness in the same way, and thus secure for his mate that chance of happiness which, ideally, is every human being's due. This, or something like it, is the resolution to which, between Ella's assault on the mask and the beginning of his prayer, between calling her a "devil woman" and calling her "the child You send me," Jim forces himself round: and by the last line—"Honey, Honey, I'll play right up to the gates of Heaven with you!"—the resolution has hardened. "Self-delusion" this is, no doubt, but a deliberately chosen, a willed, a hard-nosed and heroic self-delusion.

But this marriage which Jim preserves by his sacrifice symbolizes, too, the relations of the black and white races. Just as the "marriage" of blacks and whites in America was forced by the whites for their own profit and comfort, so Ella seeks Jim out as a husband to secure her own happiness, It is on this level, of course, that the evident symbols do their work: the stage-setting for the marriage scene; the flatiron corner, black on one side and white on the other, at the opening; the portrait of the dear Mr. Harris in his lodge regalia; and above all, the Congo mask, an object "inspiring obscure, dim connotations . . ., but beautifully done, conceived in a true religious spirit," yet acquiring, in the bourgeois, white-American setting of Jim's mother's house, a dominating, "diabolical quality."

What then are these "obscure, dim connotations"? O'Neill wrote several short pieces on the importance of masks to him as a dramatist.[6] He talks of "the soulstifling daily struggle" of people in general "to exist as masks among the masks of living." "In *All God's Chillun Got Wings,* all save the seven leading characters should be masked; for all the secondary figures are part and parcel of the Expressionistic background of the play, a world at first indifferent, then cruelly hostile, against which the tragedy of Jim Harris is outlined." O'Neill further regarded it as "unquestionable" that the new insight into "human cause and effect" provided by psychology had "uncovered the mask, . . . impressed the idea of mask as a symbol of inner reality upon all intelligent people of today." And, significantly, he included the Congo mask in a list of symbolic masks he had used in his plays. The Congo mask, then, appears to connote—or to have connoted for O'Neill— many things. Obviously, in its setting, it suggests something about the racial past of the Harris family—or the twentieth-century American conception of that past, it makes no difference which. Hattie, defiantly proud of her African heritage, regards the mask as "beautiful" and perhaps also as embodying "a true religious spirit." She stresses its value as a work of art and the "reality" of its creator as an artist. Jim is prepared, for Ella's happiness, to put this reminder of his race out of sight. And she, fascinated by it from the start, loathes it. She talks to it, saying

[6]Three pieces which first appeared in *American Spectator* (Nov. 1932, Dec. 1932, Jan. 1933) are conveniently assembled in Cargill *et al.*, pp. 116–22.

she is not afraid of it, threatening to "give it the laugh." The mixed fascination and hatred it arouses in Ella, and the stress placed on its religious meaning, suggest that it symbolizes more than just the black past. We first encounter it as a thing whose beauty has been perverted into menace by its transplantation into a twentieth-century white-bourgeois setting. As Jim wallows deeper in failure and Ella's madness grows, the mask more and more dominates the scene. So the mask means Jim's "inner reality"—his sense of failure, his blackness, and (like the Congo River in Vachel Lindsay's poem) the real primitiveness underlying the civilized aspiration and threatening the white; and it means, like the Congo River in Conrad's *Heart of Darkness,* Ella's unconscious mind, her *id*, the font of her irrational hate; and simultaneously it means the "soul-stifling struggle" of both "to exist as masks among the masks of living." And it suggests that these various referents make up a complex, a syndrome— that any one of them will at least probably accompany the others.

None of the characters is more aware of the mask as a symbol than Ella; when we view the play as an image of race relations, it is Ella's reactions to the mask that chiefly help us interpret the ending. She has, throughout Act II, been both fascinated and repelled by her own notion of her husband's racial past. That black might be beautiful, as it is for Hattie, Ella cannot and will not see—which explains why, whenever she wishes to praise Jim's kindness, honesty, or loyalty, she calls him white. She hates the notion of primitiveness which her husband's black skin and the mask both thrust upon her, and hates, in consequence, her own hateful self, the primitive *id* of which they keep reminding her. She stabs the mask because Jim's aspirations have died— because what she sees as an attempt of the black, the primitive, the *id*, to outdo and dominate her has failed. The devil is dead, and to keep him dead Jim must be kept a slave. He may serve her by living out the myth of the happy slave as her "old kind Uncle Jim." He may serve her by playing transvestive games in which she takes over from him the primitive power of blackness, that mythic power which whites have so often tried to appropriate through black-face shows, the jazz craze, slumming in Harlem, and dancing black dances. Or he may ferry her back to the innocence of her childhood, the time before she knew hatred or hated herself for knowing it.

Jim's heroic choice of self-delusion at the end of the play therefore means that the happiness of the white race in America can only be secured if the black race will deliberately seek its own happiness in serving a set of myths. It implies that there can be no settled love between whites and blacks except a perverted love purchased by the one partner's abrogation of his freedom and human dignity. It implies that the white race, in its attitudes to black people, is insane beyond cure, schizophrenic—wanting on principle to permit their advancement toward freedom, forced by its own sick nature to stifle them. If this is so, the play is indeed pessimistic; but there is one tiny note of hope at the end. Jumping excitedly to her feet as Jim prays, Ella says, "Don't cry, Jim! . . . I've only got a little time left and I want to play." Which Ella is it, one wonders, that only has "a little time left": the literal Ella; or the embodiment of race hatred as a primitive and inevitable attribute of man; or the Ella who cherishes, and imposes on the black man, the old racial myths; or simply Ella as the symbol of white dominance? In any case, there is a little hope here for all the Jim Harrises, all the Uncle Toms.

For Jim Harris is indeed an Uncle Tom. His final choice, heroic though it may be, establishes him as a Tom. Only a Tom could have used with such blindness and such ironic effect the romantic lover's metaphor of slavery to his beloved. But there surely never was a more sympathetic and provocative portrayal of the Uncle Tom than this. Jim, to be sure, is a traitor to the cause of his people, and Hattie is his foil. But Jim's words at the end of his quarrel with Hattie not only have an air of conviction but convey a deep awareness of his situation, a sense of purpose: "I have no own good. I only got a good together with her. . . . Let her call me nigger! Let her call me the whitest of the white! I'm all she's got in the world, ain't I? . . . You with your fool talk of the black race and the white race! Where does the human race get a chance to come in? I suppose that's simple for you. You lock it up in asylums and throw away the key!" The tragedy of Jim Harris is that he is an Uncle Tom not out of fear or the desire for comfort, but out of love even more catholic than Hattie's, and that this love inescapably drags him into willing on himself a lifelong humiliation.

From *Thirst* (1914) through *The Moon of the Caribbees, The Dreamy Kid,* and *The Emperor Jones* to *All God's Chillun* we can trace a gradual change in O'Neill's treatment of the black American. The Negro Sailor in that implausible play *Thirst* is a savage who, once civilization is out of sight, will cheerfully cannibalize a dead body. Of course he is also a noble savage who patiently bears the slanders of his white companions and spurns with quiet dignity not only their threats but also their bribes and the woman's tawdry enticements. He is also not very bright. If there were any black people in the audience at the play's first night at Provincetown in 1916 they might well have seen in it a stupid insult to themselves, a contribution to a set of dangerous stereotypes.[7]

The Moon of the Caribbees is much more subtle, and its subtlety has encouraged white critics to play down its racial meaning. Barrett Clark calls it "a fairly successful attempt to suggest certain sensations through the use of rhythmical prose— not alone the spirit of the sea, but of man's loneliness in the presence of nature. . . . There is practically no story in it."[8] And in general it has been interpreted as an atmosphere piece. Yet it has quite as much story as atmosphere, and more story than many one-act plays. Under the irrational moon, to the sound of a primitive death-chant, some sailors representative of modern Western civilization are visited by a group of women from the land whence the chant emanates. Like Pan and Dionysus, the black women bring sex and liquor, under whose influence the civilization of the sailors is stripped away. They quarrel in the moonlight, they fight like satyrs, and a man is nearly sacrificed. Clearly the play states, in small compass but powerfully, an idea of man's nature which had been plausible since Darwin, Freud, Frazer, and the early works of Jung. But by using black characters and a black artifact—the song—to represent the primitive it becomes ambiguous in an unfortunate way. At the same time, *The Moon* modifies the view of O'Neill that *Thirst* may have given us: at any rate it makes *Thirst* look a little less like anti-black propaganda.

Of *The Dreamy Kid* (1919) Clark says, "This play about negroes is not one of the best: it is too obvious, too direct and melodramatic to be wholly convincing. It is the story of a murderer pursued by the police, who returns to see his dying mother [sic] and gets caught."[9] And that is all: the play contains nothing about race and superstition, apparently, and the totemic figure of the grandmother, the dread of whose curse makes the Kid, an urban black, pass up a chance of escape and stay at her deathbed to fight a gun-battle with the police, has even, by a Freudian slip,

[7]The play was only once published, in *Thirst and Other One-Act Plays* (American Dramatists' Series, Boston, 1914), a collection which O'Neill later repudiated entirely: Barrett H. Clark, *Eugene O'Neill: The Man and His Plays* (New York, 1929), pp. 66–67.

[8]Clark, pp. 83–84.

[9]Clark, p. 92.

become the American mom. *The Dreamy Kid* is, in fact, a touchy play. Perhaps it portrays the residue of primitive superstition in civilized man; but perhaps its statement is only about the *black* man, perhaps it is a restatement of a popular racial myth. In any case, it well illustrates the impossibility of conveying a universal statement through a black character.

A well-known Anglo-Jewish writer once remarked that, as a Jew, he sometimes felt sick after hearing a Wagner music-drama, not because the music had seemed ugly but because it had intoxicated him, sucked him in, stirred in him a complex of emotions he would rather not have known himself capable of. The effect of *The Emperor Jones* is perhaps something like this, though whether the spectator feels any disgust afterwards, and how great the disgust is, will depend probably on his race, his upbringing, and the reality and depth of certain of his professed beliefs. The play foreshadows the complexities of *All God's Chillun* and at the same time presents again, more starkly, the ambivalence of *The Moon* and *The Dreamy Kid*. Is Brutus Jones an image of all mankind? Is he made black only because, in the days when Darwin and Jung smelt headier than they do now, any black man might seem, whatever his early environment and experiences, closer than the white to the common ancestry of both? Or is he an image only of his race? The comments of many white critics, even the best-intentioned of them, show how unfortunate is this ambivalence. "*The Emperor Jones* is a magnificent presentment of panic fear in the breast of a half-civilized negro." "It is a kind of unfolding, in reverse order, of the tragical epic of the American negro." The moon "casts its doubtful light on scenes of re-enacted memory—partly from the actual past of Jones's life, and partly from the racial past of the Negro people." Jones is "reclaimed by the primitive ancestral savagery that had spawned and doomed him." In the operatic version, Lawrence Tibbett as Jones "dominated the proceedings from the moment that he appeared, blustering, insolent, preposterous . . . until, an abject and ghost-ridden savage, praying, pleading, whimpering, and hysterical, shorn of his thin caking of sophistication, he shot himself [sic] . . . an atavistic sacrifice."[10] That Darwinian-Jungian word "atavistic" pounds through the reviews as monotonously as the tom-tom in the play: one critic burbled of "the rhythmic frenzy of his atavistic terrors, as he stumbles through the jungle night back to the darkness of his ancestral savagery." "Regression" and

[10]Clark, p. 105; ibid., p. 104; review by Lawrence Gilman in *New York Herald Tribune* (Jan. 8, 1933), in Carpenter, p. 90.

"reversion," too, appear with tiring frequency.[11] Richard D. Skinner tries to argue that Jones is a symbol of mankind: he is made black only in order to indicate the nature of the individual soul's struggle with pride: "it is not a question of superiority or inferiority of race, but of the historical symbol which the negro has become through centuries of bondage."[12] But Skinner's is a lonely voice: people's recorded reactions do not bear him out. The equivocal nature of this impressive play is beautifully illustrated in a comment by Oscar Cargill, who calls it "a study of the involuntary regression of an individual consciousness through the stages of its own history to the racial or collective unconscious."[13] Racial, or collective? If we only knew, we could feel more comfortable in applauding *The Emperor Jones*.

The same ambiguity, then, runs through all the "negro plays" up to *Jones;* but as their meanings become more important, their technique more sure, their characters more credible, the ambiguity becomes more teasing and the possibility of interpreting them as propagandistic or myth-serving plays grow less. In *All God's Chillun,* not only did O'Neill succeed in creating more credible black characters still; he almost succeeded in so presenting his themes—primitivism, race prejudice, superstition, and so forth—that the kind of uncomfortable ambiguity we have seen in the earlier plays should exist only in the eye of the beholder. Or rather, Jim and Hattie are so human that the reader refusing to see them as stereotypes out of a racist myth, is inclined to attribute to Ella's diseased mind the notion of ineradicable primitiveness conveyed in the symbolism.

The last stage in the progession is *The Iceman Cometh* (1946), a play with only one black character, and he merely one of the eighteen down-and-out habitués of Harry Hope's "End of the Line Café." Joe Mott's blackness contributes nothing to the plays thematic development. He objects, certainly, to being called a nigger, and declares himself essentially white; but these utterances have to be seen only as indications, the one of Mott's remaining pride in himself, the other of the particular kind of impotence and blindness which have helped bring him to Hope's

[11]Gilman; and see, e.g., the excerpts from Isaac Goldberg and Andrew E. Malone in Cargill *et al.* (pp. 236, 240, 259) and Maida Castellun's *New York Call* (Nov. 10, 1920) repr. in Jordan Y. Miller, ed., *Playwright's Progress: O'Neill and the Critics* (Chicago, 1965), p. 23.

[12]*Eugene O'Neill: A Poet's Quest* (New York, 1964), p. 86.

[13]"Fusion-Point of Jung and Nietzsche," in Cargill *et al.*, p. 408, n. Noteworthy too is Malone's remark: "whereas the primitiveness of Jones is spiritual, that of Yank [in *The Hairy Ape*] is entirely physical." (Cargill *et al.*, p. 261).

limbo for the blind and impotent. But as the black critic John Lovell, Jr., wrote soon after the play came out, Joe Mott suddenly seems an important character—important not only in this play, but in O'Neill's whole output, in American drama, indeed in American history—when we look at him as the last of the series of portraits that began with the Sailor in *Thirst*.[14] Lovell underestimates *All God's Chillun* as a stage in O'Neill's development as a creator of black characters, seeing it as an advance only in that its author was the first white American dramatist to present "the lowliest American aspiring to the loftiest American ideals." But on the significance, in this development, of *The Iceman Cometh* Lovell is resoundingly right. Joe Mott's significance, he says, is not in the psychological accuracy of his portrayal. One theme of *The Iceman* is aspiration and failure: like the other dead-beats, Joe has aspired; like theirs, his soul has died because "his aspiration was not good enough." "Thus Joe Mott is given equality of struggle, aspiration, and failure, according to his constitutional rights. None of the equalities is more terribly important. . . . The macabre stage at the end . . . has greater meaning than usual because here, for once in America, . . . a Negro has aspired and died on terms of equality."

Mary Welch, the actress, once drew O'Neill into conversation on his "negro plays." "He had felt deeply about them, and his face grew bitter and forceful as he recalled how some of the New York theatre crowd had accepted these works." In his own words, "They didn't really understand what I was writing. They merely said to themselves, 'Oh look, the ape can talk!' "[15] But there are several causes for the misunderstanding, two of them attributable to O'Neill himself.

One cause, of course, was a prevalent attitude among white Americans toward black Americans—not the Ku Klux Klan attitude, nor even that of the *avant-garde* of the jazz age, but that of the ordinary, well-meaning "liberal" white, who tended, as we have seen, to be caught with his super-ego down by plays like *The Emperor Jones* and to try to read *All God's Chillun* as a tragedy of love and marriage. Another cause, though a lesser one, was the spirit of the black movements of the day. Blacks reacted just as vehemently to *All God's Chillun* as whites did, feeling that it reflected unfavorably on their race, and the black reaction to the "negro plays" in general was hostile because they pre-

---

[14]"Eugene O'Neill's Darker Brother," *Theatre Arts* 32 (Feb., 1948), 45–48.
[15]"Softer Tones for Mr. O'Neill's Portrait," *Theatre Arts* 41 (May, 1957), p. 82.

sented the black man as an unfortunate creature in sordid circumstances. Four months after the first night of *All God's Chillun*, William Stanley Braithwaite, a black critic not normally
given to vehement condemnations, published an article attacking
O'Neill, among others, for giving a defamatory picture of black
Americans, for dramatizing "the sordid aspects of life and unde-
sirable types of character." Though Braithwaite was right, probably, in finding O'Neill and other white writers incapable of
presenting "the immense paradox of racial life" because their
culture limited them to a conception of the black American as "in-
ferior, superstitious, half-ignorant," still, when he objects to
O'Neill's and Ernest Culbertson's plays that "the best and highest class of racial life has not yet been discovered for literary
treatment by white American authors," he betrays an attitude to
literature comparable to that of Lenin or the more moralistic Victorian critics.[16] One wonders how Braithwaite would have responded to *The Iceman Cometh* twenty-two years later—or, for
that matter, to Wright's *Native Son*.

To add to the misunderstanding, O'Neill himself was not
especially coherent in talking about his own plays: the plays may
be fundamentally equivocal, but O'Neill's intellect was apparently less capable than his imagination of framing clear state-
ments about racial issues. He repeatedly tried, in response to the
muddled and misdirected criticism of *All God's Chillun*, to represent the racial issues in the play as merely incidental, and Jim and
Ella as symbolizing nothing beyond themselves—a hopelessly un-
tenable position, of course, since no reader or spectator could be
expected to do such violence to his own response-system as
O'Neill seems to demand.[17]

The most important cause of misunderstanding, however,
lies in the plays themselves. It is the notion, distilled from an
atmosphere full of Darwin, Frazer, and Jung—full of "atavism,"
"regression," and "the racial unconscious"—that the black
American carried in his heredity a deeper shade of the Congo
jungle, louder echoes of the witch-doctor's rattle, a livelier response to totems and funeral chants, than his white neighbors. To
this suggestion white readers and spectators responded, generally, with glee. Their black counterparts, unable to change the prevalent intellectual scheme, either sidestepped the idea or, as did
the Harlem Renaissance writers, adapted it to different ends.
They had to wait until 1940, when Richard Wright supplied, in

[16]"The Negro in Literature," *Crisis* 28 (Sept., 1924), 204–10.
[17]See, e.g., the quotation in Arthur and Barbara Gelb, pp. 535–36.

Bigger Thomas, a motivation for the crime and defiance of the Dreamy Kid, for the Negro Sailor's access to life at the death of the white woman, for the flight of Jones—a motivation more credible and, uncomfortably, closer to home.

Nonetheless, O'Neill achieved much in these plays. Only in one very early and trifling play—one which, in fairness to him, should probably be left in the obscurity he consigned it to—did he ever succumb to any of the crudest racial myths. The predominant myth in the plays up to *Jones*, the myth of the black man as primitive, was not merely popular but had after all much scientific sanction. O'Neill wrote no *Leopard's Spots,* no *Birth of a Nation,* but instead worked his way gradually towards a sympathetic and imaginative presentation of the black American's blackness, towards presenting blackness as a subjective phenomenon. Having reached, or nearly reached, this goal in *All God's Chillun,* he admittedly failed to go a step further; he might reasonably, for instance, have explored further the predicament which made an Uncle Tom of Jim Harris, or have examined more closely the social and psychological barriers to black equality. Instead, discouraged apparently by the perversity of his audiences, he abandoned black characters for twenty years. But at least, by 1924, he had developed the courage and insight to represent the white American response to blackness as diseased and degraded, and further than that no white writer of the time could probably be expected to have advanced.

Roger Asselineau

Desire under the Elms
A Phase of Eugene O'Neill's Philosophy

Though to all appearances O'Neill was primarily a playwright and an experimenter with dramatic forms who never considered himself a thinker, he was in fact desperately trying to
express "something" in all his plays. He chose drama as a me-
dium, but, for all his interest in technique, he never considered it
an end in itself, but rather a means to live by proxy a certain
number of problems which obsessed him. In *Lazarus Laughed*, he
speaks of men as "those haunted heroes." Actually this is less a
definition of mankind than a description of himself. He composed
plays because he *had* to write in order to liberate himself and exor-
cise ghosts. It was a compulsion. The result was plays because of
his environment, because his father was an actor and he was an
"enfant de la balle," but it might have been novels just as well,
and he would probably have written better novels than plays, for
he was constantly hampered by the limitations of the stage. In his
case literary creation was not a gratuitous activity, but an intense
imaginative experience, an *"Erlebnis."* He lived it. It was a passionate answer to the problems which tormented him with ex-
cruciating strength. This is no mere figure of speech. He roamed
the world for years in search of a solution, trying to find a remedy
for his fundamental despair, giving up the comfort and security of
family life and nearly losing his health and life in the process.

After his wandering years, his *Wanderjahre,* when his health
broke down and he was obliged to bring his restless comings-
and-goings to a close, he went on exploring the world in imagination, not as a dilettante or a tourist in the realms of thought, but as
a passionate pilgrim in quest of a shrine at which to worship.
Though brought up a Roman Catholic, he lost his faith as an
adolescent. Yet his nature abhorred this spiritual vacuum and he

From Festschrift Rudolf Stamm, *edited by Eduard Kolb and Jörg
Hasler, 1969. Reprinted by permission of Francke Verlag, Bern, Switzer-
land.*

ardently looked for a substitute ever after. His religious faith was killed by rationalism and scientific materialism, but the restlessness and violence of his quest for a personal religion sprang from no coldly rational intellect.

Each of his plays is thus not only an experiment in craftsmanship, but also an attempt to find God or at least some justification for the flagrant inconsistencies of the human condition. His interest was less in psychology than in metaphysics. He said so himself in a letter to Joseph Wood Krutch: "Most modern plays are concerned with the relation between man and man, but that does not interest me at all. I am interested only in the relation between man and God."[1]

In spite of its apparent dramatic directness therefore, *Desire under the Elms* is essentially, like his other plays, a philosophical tragedy about man and God rather than a naturalistic chunk of life depicting the mores of a bunch of clumsy New England rustics.

Reduced to essentials in this very primitive setting man appears primarily as an animal. The first specimens whom we have a chance to observe when the curtain rises, Eben and especially Simeon and Peter, look like oxen, eat, work and behave like a team of oxen, and feel tied up to the other animals of the farm by bonds of brotherhood: "... the cows knows us ... An' the hosses, an' pigs, an' chickens ... They knows us like brothers— and likes us"[2] (Part I, scene 4). They obey their instincts blindly and think only of drinking, eating and fornicating. Their lust is quite literally bestial as is shown by Eben's account of his visit to Min: "I begun t'beller like a calf an' cuss at the same time . . . an' she got scared, an' I just grabbled holt an' tuk her"[3] (Part I, scene 3). When Abbie courts Eben, the scene is not much different. She kisses him greedily and at first he submits dumbly, but soon, after returning her kisses he hurls her away from him and, O'Neill tells us, "they stand speechless and breathless, panting like two animals"[4] (Part II, scene 2).

These inarticulate, animal-like creatures differ from their dumb brothers in only one respect (but it is hardly an improvement): they are possessed with the mania of owning things, whether gold or land. They all crave for money or title-deeds. In short, they bear a strong family likeness to Swift's Yahoos. They have only one redeeming feature: an embryonic sense of beauty

[1]Quoted by Joseph Wood Krutch in his introduction to the Modern Library Edition of O'Neill's *Nine Plays*, p. xvii.

[2]Ibid., p. 152.

[3]Ibid., p. 148.

[4]Ibid., p. 174.

which makes them exclaim "purty" in a rather monotonous manner whenever they notice the beauty of their surroundings. The only exception is the sheriff, who at the very end of the play passes very matter-of-fact and anti-climactic comments on the salable value of the farm while Eben and Abbie admire the beauty of the sunrise.

Far from being a free agent, man is thus by and large the slave of his instincts and O'Neill here revives the old Calvinistic dogma of predestination. As early as his very first play, *The Web,* of the transparent title, he attempted to show that man is caught in a web of circumstances, a web that is not of his own weaving. At the end of *The Web,* O'Neill tells us that Rose, the prostitute, "seems to be aware of something in the room which none of the others can see—perhaps the personification of the ironic life force that has crushed her."[5] In *Desire under the Elms* Eben feels trapped in exactly the same way: "Each day," the stage directions inform us, "is a cage in which he finds himself trapped."[6] He is indeed trapped by circumstances—tied up to that bleak New England farm which he somehow considers part of his mother, and he is also psychologically trapped by an all-powerful mother-complex which unknown to him determines his whole behavior towards his father as well as towards women in general. His temperament is wholly determined by his heredity: it is a combination of his mother's softness and lack of will, as his father again and again points out, and of his father's aggressiveness and obstinacy, as his two elder brothers repeatedly tell us: "he is a chip off the old block, the spitting image of his father. ..."

As to Abbie, she is just as trapped as he is. When she enters the stage, we are warned that she has "the same unsettled, untamed, desperate quality which is so apparent in Eben."[7] And shortly afterwards we learn that she "was a orphan early an' had t'wuk fur others in other folks' hums" and her first husband "turned out a drunken spreer" and got sick and died. She then felt free again only to discover that all she was free for was to work again "in other folks' hums, doin' other folks' wuk" till she had almost given up hope of ever doing her own work in her own home[8] (Part I, scene 4).

Ephraim Cabot himself, for all his will-power and vigor, is caught in the same web as the others. His whole behavior is

[5]*Ten Lost Plays* (New York, Random House, 1964), p. 53.
[6]*Nine Plays,* p. 137.
[7]Ibid., p. 155.
[8]Ibid., p. 160.

conditioned by his Puritan upbringing. He cannot think of anything but work, hard work on a barren New England farm.
"Laborare est orare," Carlyle claimed, "work is worship." Ephraim Cabot is a degenerate Puritan. Work has ceased to be a
form of worship for him, yet he believes in its virtue and absolute
value because he has been brought up that way. He once tried to
escape this self-imposed serfdom. Like many other New England-
ers, he went West and in the broad meadows of the central
plains found black soil as rich as gold, without a stone. He had
only to plough and sow and then sit and smoke his pipe and watch
things grow. He could have become a rich man and led an easy
and idle life, but he preferred to give it up and return to his New
England farm and to hard work on a stony soil,[9] which proves the
extraordinary strength of his Puritan compulsions. They practically deprived him of his freedom of choice.

So, at the start at least, the three major characters of *Desire
under the Elms* are not free. They bear psychological or moral
chains. Consequently, they cannot be held responsible for their
actions and Simeon with his peasant shrewdness is perfectly
aware of it. When Eben accuses his father of killing his "Maw,"
Simeon retorts: "No one never kills nobody. It's allus somethin'
that's the murderer"[10] (Part I, scene 2). "Somethin'," that is to
say one of those mysterious things which impel men to act this
way or that, whether they like it or not, whether they are aware of
it or not. This is a modified form of Puritan pessimism: all men
are sinners in the clutches of Satan—or of God who is always
"nagging his sheep to sin"[11] (Part I, scene 4), the better to punish
them afterwards, always ready to smite his undutiful sons with
His worst curse.

How can a man save his soul under such circumstances?
Though, theoretically, O'Neill's approach is strictly non-
theological and he is not concerned with the problem of salvation,
he is constantly obsessed with it all the same and in this particular
play, he gives it a Nietzschean answer: passion. Passion alone, he
suggests, can enable man to transcend his animal nature. He
repeatedly exalts the purity and transfiguring power of love.
Eben's passion for Abbie which at first is mere lust soon becomes
love—and there is a difference in kind between the two. The
passage from lust to love is similar to the transmutation of lead
into gold. Whereas lust, which is tied to the body, is finite and
transient, love, which transcends the body, is infinite and eternal.

[9]Ibid., p. 172.
[10]Ibid., p. 141.
[11]Ibid., p. 161.

Abbie kills her infant son to prove her love to Eben, and at the end of scene 3 of Part III proclaims that her love for Eben will never change, whatever he does to her. The play ends on an apotheosis of love. The two lovers stand "looking up raptly in attitudes strangely aloof and devout" at the "purty" rising sun, which contrasts with the pallid setting sun that lit up the opening of the play, at a time when everything took place on the plane of coarse material things and lust.

Man can thus be redeemed by a great passion and save his soul and attain grandeur. The farm under the elms, which looked so sordid when the curtain rose, witnesses a sublime *dénouement* and at the end almost becomes one of those places where the spirit bloweth.

The reason for this extraordinary change is that, in Hamlet's words:

> There are more things in heaven and earth . . .
> Than are dreamt of in all [our] philosophy,

as Cabot again and again feels, for all his hardness and insensitivity: "They's thin's pokin' about in the dark—in the corners"[12] (Part II, scene 2). "Even the music can't drive it out—somethin'. Ye kin feel it droppin' off the elums, climbin' up the roof, sneakin' down the chimney, pokin' in the corners. They's no peace in houses, they's no rest livin' with folks. Somethin's always livin' with ye. . . ."[13] (Part III, scene 2).

What is that "somethin' " whose presence disturbs him? It is the "Desire" of the title—an irresistible life-force (somewhat similar to G. B. Shaw's), which flows through the elms and through old Cabot himself sometimes, as when it makes him leave his farm in spring and go in search of a new wife. But it is especially powerful in Eben and Abbie. It is that thing which makes Eben look like a wild animal in captivity when he enters the stage and feel "inwardly unsubdued." It is quite impersonal and Eben refers to it in the neuter: "I kin feel it growin' in me—growin' an' growin'—till it'll bust out"[14] (Part I, scene 2). It is the magnetic force which draws Eben to Abbie through walls and partitions (Part II, scene 2). It is Nature—and Abbie intones a hymn to her—or it—in her own inarticulate way when she presses Eben to yield to his passion: "Hain't the sun strong an' hot? Ye kin feel it burnin' into the earth—Nature—makin' thin's grow—bigger 'n'

[12]Ibid., p. 174.
[13]Ibid., p. 189.
[14]Ibid., p. 144.

bigger—burnin' inside ye—makin' ye want t'grow—into somethin' else—till ye are jined with it—an' it's your'n—but it owns
ye—too—an' makes ye grow bigger—like a tree—like them
elums"[15] (Part II, scene 1).

In short, the "Desire" which flows through the elms and
drips from them and pervades everything under them is God—
though the word is never used. It is not, however, the God of the
Christians, but rather a dynamic, impersonal, pantheistic or
panpsychistic deity present in all things, whether animate or in-
animate, breaking barriers between individuals as in the case of
Eben and Abbie, dissolving their lonesomeness and making them
feel one. In a way it is a pagan God, a Dionysian deity, for it
partly manifests itself in the form of carnal desire. Under its
influence, Eben and Cabot become inspired poets (in prose) and
sing woman, the lovely incarnation of the soft and warm goddess
of fertility and life: "She's like t'night, she's soft 'n' warm, her
eyes kin wink like a star, her mouth's wa'm, her arms're wa'm. She
smells like a wa'm plowed field, she's purty"[16] (Part I, scene 2).
"Yew air my Rose o' Sharon! Behold! yew air fair; yer eyes
air doves; yer lips air like scarlet; yer two breasts air like two
fawns; yer navel be like a round goblet; yer belly be like a heap
o' wheat," exclaims old Cabot echoing chapters 4 and 7 of the
Song of Solomon.[17]

This omnipresent God is fundamentally a cosmic sexual
urge, spontaneous, beautiful, unselfish and amoral. In this
perspective the notion of sin becomes meaningless. "He was the
child of our sin," says Eben of the baby, but Abbie proudly
answers "as if defying God" (the God of the Christians): "I
don't repent that sin. I ain't askin' God t'fergive that"[18] (Part III,
scene 4). The two lovers have gone back to the Garden of Eden
from which Adam and Eve were expelled. They have become
"Children of Adam," to take up Walt Whitman's phrase.

The life-force, the desire which circulates through the elms
as well as through the *dramatis personae* is the very reverse of
the God worshipped by Ephraim Cabot, which has the hardness
and immobility of a stone—and the sterility of one (Part II, scene
2). His God is the God of repression and lonesomeness and hard
work—the God humorously called up by Robert Frost in "Of the

[15]Ibid., p. 164.
[16]Ibid., p. 145.
[17]Ibid., p. 167.
[18]Ibid., p. 203.

Stones of the Place" and to some extent a duplicate of Robinson Jeffers's anti-human God.

Abbie, on the contrary, recommends to yield to the life impulse, to let Nature speak at every hazard "without check with original energy."[19] It is against nature, it is impious, she claims, to resist its will: "It's agin nature, Eben. Ye been fightin' yer nature ever since the day I come. . . ."[20] (Part II, scene 1).

This is a combination of Nietzsche's Dionysian philosophy and Freudianism and in *Desire under the Elms* it leads—in spite of the Dostoevskian quality of the *Crime and Punishment* situation at the end of the play—to an optimistic conclusion: the couple Eben–Abbie is not crushed by adverse circumstances. They have fulfilled themselves, they have fully lived and, far from being driven to despair by their trials, they are full of a strange "hopeless hope" when the curtain falls.

In this play we thus witness the dramatic clash of two opposite philosophies: Old Cabot's Puritanism and Abbie's worship of Dionysus—a conflict between the stones of the former and the elms of the latter, which O'Neill himself seems to have experienced throughout his life. He obviously sympathized with warm uninhibited characters like Eben and Abbie in *Desire under the Elms* and with Marie Brantôme and Christine in *Mourning Becomes Electra,* though he never was warm and uninhibited himself. In everyday life, except when he was under the influence of alcohol, he was to some extent closer to Cabot than to Eben. Other things being equal, he suffered from the same dichotomy as Dr. Jekyll. Two men were at war within him. He was both Billy Brown and Dion Anthony. But the twain never fused. He was probably thinking of his own predicament when he made Dion, "life's lover," complain in *The Great God Brown* "with a suffering bewilderment": "Why am I afraid to dance, I who love music and rhythm and grace and song and laughter? Why am I afraid to live, I who love life and the beauty of flesh and the living colors of the earth and sky and sea? Why am I afraid of love, I who love love? . . . Why must I be so ashamed of my strength, so proud of my weakness?"[21] (Prologue). He would have liked freely to worship "the Great God Pan,"[22] as Dion calls him, instead of that he

[19] Walt Whitman, "Song of Myself," *Leaves of Grass,* section 1, l.13.
[20] *Nine Plays,* p. 164.
[21] Ibid., p. 315.
[22] Ibid., p. 318.

had to bear "the intolerable chalice of life."[23] He would have liked to laugh with Lazarus and shout like Lazarus's followers:

> There is only life,
> There is only laughter[24]   (Act II, scene 1),

but his ingrained masochistic catholicism made laughter die on his lips. *Desire under the Elms* is the secret expression of his poignant nostalgia for a joy of life which he was unable to experience.

However, his personal failure and his acute awareness of the cruelty of the human condition did not prevent him from concluding that life is a vivid and exciting experience well worth the trouble to the very end. And that is why Abbie and Eben do not commit suicide in the last act and even Lavinia refuses to kill herself in *Mourning Becomes Electra*, thus breaking one of the most imperative laws of tragedy. O'Neill's ultimate attitude to life during this nostalgic period (1923 to 1926) is best expressed by the hero of *The Great God Brown:* "I've loved, lusted, won and lost, sung and wept"[25] (Act II, scene 2). And anyway, as O'Neill proclaimed in *Lazarus Laughed* in conformity with Nietzsche's teachings: "Men are ... unimportant ... Man remains ... For Man death is not." The same life-force flows through all men and whatever their personal limitations may be, whether they are bums, drunken sailors or New England farmers, it endows them all with tragic *grandeur*. All individuals are potentially as worthy of interest as the mighty kings and queens of Greek tragedies. *Desire under the Elms* is thus the quiet affirmation of the fundamental dignity of all men in a godless (?) universe—or at least in a universe deprived of the help and support of the personal God posited by Christianity.

[23]Ibid., p. 375.
[24]Ibid., p. 418.
[25]Ibid., p. 347.

Otis W. Winchester

Eugene O'Neill's Strange Interlude *as a Transcript of America in the 1920's*

> Rather more in the 1920's than in other periods did books clearly
> establish the inevitability of their inclusion in an adequate history of
> the times. An author might take refuge in an ivory tower to avoid
> the rub of the world, yet he could not help reflecting the world.
> Even less could he avoid influencing it.[1]

The connection between history and literature to which
Mark Sullivan alludes is clearer still when applied specifically to
drama of the era. Eugene O'Neill's *Strange Interlude,* heralded
in 1928 as "not only the supreme novelty of the play season, but
also as the most significant drama so far written by an American,"[2] is a remarkable metaphorical description of America's
"strange interlude," the 1920's, reflecting and influencing the
period as profoundly as any literary work of the day.

Its great length and the interior monologue were certainly
novel and undoubtedly contributed to *Strange Interlude*'s popularity. The performance began at five-thirty in the afternoon and
recessed at a quarter to eight, for dinner, and resumed at nine for
slightly more than two hours. The characters spoke some of their
thoughts aloud, not as asides or soliloquy but as something approaching stream-of-consciousness. The Theater Guild's greatest
success, *Strange Interlude* opened at the John Golden Theater,
New York, on January 30, 1928, and ran for 426 performances.
Several companies toured with the play, all meeting with success.
The first printing of *Strange Interlude,* twenty thousand copies,
sold quickly and for months it held its place as a national best-
seller. The movie version of *Strange Interlude*, released in late
summer of 1932, was highly publicized, given a lavish Hollywood

[1]Mark Sullivan, *Our Time: The Twenties* (New York: Charles Scribners Sons,
1935), p. 322.
[2]Burns Mantle, *American Playwrights of Today* (New York: Dodd, Mead and
Co., 1929), p. 18.

From Literature and History, *edited by I. E. Cadenhead, Jr., 1970.
Reprinted by permission of the University of Tulsa.*

première, and considered the cinema event of the year.—All this enhances the significance of *Strange Interlude* for the social historian, who is likely to be more interested in public response to an *Uncle Tom's Cabin* than in scholarly appreciations of its literary values.

Very briefly, the story of *Strange Interlude* is Nina's. A woman of passionate temperament is inhibited and dominated by the sterile philosophy of her father. Gordon Shaw, her fiancé, represents fulfillment and escape but is killed in the war. Nina gradually realizes that it was her father's influence that prevented the marriage or at least a physical consummation which would have lessened the intensity of her loss. Frustrated sexually and maternally, guilty with a sense of having failed her fiancé, and recoiling from the anathema of her father's Puritanism, Nina attempts to find expiation and fulfillment through masochistically giving herself physically to wounded war veterans. When this fails, the guilt and frustration increase. On the advice of Dr. Darrell, she marries a shallow and uncomplicated businessman, Sam Evans, and attempts to escape introspective suffering through becoming a wife and mother. Nina's adjustment is prevented by her mother-in-law's disclosure that the Evans family is cursed with hereditary insanity and her insistence that she have a secret abortion. Although sacrificing herself to make Sam happy, Nina is confronted by both her own maternal frustration and her husband's fear of sterility. As an answer to the dilemma, she arranges to secretly have a child by another man, as Mrs. Evans had suggested. Dr. Darrell, the accomplice, and Nina fall in love but cannot marry without destroying Evans. Darrell goes abroad in self-imposed exile. Nina achieves a degree of contentment with her husband and young son he believes to be his. Through her relationship with four men, Marsden (a father surrogate), Darrell (her lover), Evans (her husband), and Gordon (her son and virtual reincarnation of Gordon Shaw), Nina eventually attains a momentary sense of the complete fulfillment of feminine desires. Gradually she loses them, Darrell through the waning of passion, Evans in death, and Gordon to another woman. Only Marsden remains and Nina, exhausted by the "fight for happiness,"[3] turns to him as a symbol of the security and peace of childhood.

Strange Interlude is in some respects typical of protest literature written during the 1920's. Although the static qualities of the economic and political order and the general loss of interest in reform and idealism tend to suggest otherwise, the decade was

[3]Eugene O'Neill, *Nine Plays by Eugene O'Neill* (New York: Random House, n.d.), p. 619. Hereafter page references to this edition will appear in the text.

one of active social revolution. At least a significant number of intellectuals were clearly disturbed by the persistence well into the 20th century of Victorian manners and morals, medieval economics, and Rousseauistic idealism. And a relatively small group of writers, the "Lost Generation" as they came to be called, influenced the entire decade of the 1920's with their disillusionment, sense of frustration, cynicism, Byronic self-consciousness, and romantic self-pity. Disillusioned first about the war and its ideals of glory, honor, courage, and sacrifice, they began to investigate other aspects of contemporary life and found much of it no less empty.

But O'Neill is very likely a more profound student of social history than many of his contemporaries who were openly didactic and propagandistic. The matters which incited most writers to take part in the agitation for social change are, for him, symbols of a deeper dilemma. O'Neill's conception of this condition which underlies and unifies the specific problems of human existence is particularly clear in *Strange Interlude*. O'Neill suggests that Modern man, emerging into the Scientific-Materialistic stage in his social development, is beyond the solace of either Primitive innocence or Puritan pride. Aware of the self-effacing truth of the former status and of the egocentric need for the latter, he is beset by unrelenting tension and suffering. For this "sickness of today," as he once termed it, O'Neill prescribes no easy cures. But this loss of the sense of belonging is not a problem of the 20's alone.

The same aura of somnolence and change, of tremendous trivia and social revolution, of reaction and counter reaction that pervaded the 1920's hovers over *Strange Interlude*. In particular the play reflects public attitude—always an illusive quantity for the social historian—toward several prominent controversies of the day: psychoanalysis, theological and ethical questioning, and rampant hedonism; the period's proclivity for mass producing heroes; and the failure of business, science, and art to fulfill either their promise or their responsibility.

Mark Sullivan relates that people "went by the thousands to take Eugene O'Neill's five-hour lesson in psychopathology, *Strange Interlude*."[4]

> What is his speciality?... neurologist, I think... I hope not a psychoanalyst... a lot to account for, Herr Freud!... punishment to fit his crimes, be forced to listen eternally during breakfast while innumberable plain ones tell him dreams about snakes... pah, what an easy

[4]Sullivan, *Our Time: The Twenties*, p. 393.

cure-all! ... sex the philosopher's stone ... O Oedipus, O my King!
The world is adopting you! ... (p. 516).

Marsden's statement contains the only direct reference to Freud
and his theories in *Strange Interlude*. It suggests the cult-like
popularity psychoanalysis attained during the period but does
not indicate the extent to which that concept of human personality
was utilized throughout the play both as a principal theme and as
fundamental to the basic dramatic conception.

Psychoanalytic theory has been a major idea of the 20th century, possibly the most important influence upon literature and
social behavior of any single philosophy of scientific deter-
minism. While the circulation of the idea in America began about
1909, when Freud and Jung lectured at Clark University, the real
penetration of psychoanalytic thought took place during the
1920's. Freud and Jung were themselves, however, read very
little and understood even less. So the psychoanalytic theory
which eventually did become incorporated into popular thought
had been "filtered through successive minds of interpreters and
popularizers and guileless readers and people who had heard
guileless readers talk about it."[5] And O'Neill functioned as one
of these "popularizers."

For a generation in revolt against lingering 19th century
manners and morals, the synthesis of Freud and Jung it discovered in *Strange Interlude* offered a compelling rationale. From
Freud come notions about the primacy of the sexual drive, the
relation of inner conflict to neurosis, the psychological insight
afforded through dreams and slips of the tongue, and the form
taken by neurotic symptoms: Nina's neurosis is, for example,
largely the product of frustrated sexual and related maternal
drives. Her relationships with all the men of the play are clearly
of a sexual basis. The guilt and repressions with which Marsden
struggles throughout much of the play are apparently the result of
a conflict between immature and mature sexual motives. Darrell's personality disorientation is a product of sexual frustration.
Even Sam Evans, who is freest of any neurotic tendency, is for a
time incapacitated by fear of sterility.

The idea that inner conflict was the cause of neurosis is
generally associated with psychoanalysis. Certainly, Darrell's
personal struggle illustrates the psychoanalytic interpretation of
inner conflict very clearly. He desires Nina sexually, he is ration-
ally aware of the unsettling effect this attachment will have upon

[5]Frederick Lewis Allen, *Only Yesterday* (New York: Harper and Bros., 1931),
p. 99.

his career and scientific principles, and he is conscious of a sense of honor and duty which forbids it. The three-way pattern in the conflict—between the id, ego, and superego—is here and elsewhere quite pointed. The interior monologue, with its attempt to penetrate the surface of the characters and to demonstrate the conflict between the spoken and silent thought, and between conscious and unconscious processes, is probably the most distinctly psychoanalytic gesture in *Strange Interlude*. Indeed, much of it is apparently intended to suggest the uncensored speech of the analyst's couch.

Dreams and slips of the tongue, valued by psychoanalysts as insights into unconscious motives and by 1928 the subject of considerable popular interest, are prominent in *Strange Interlude*: Marsden's dreams are largely concerned with his suppressed sexuality; Nina's, more richly symbolic, are products of her guilt and insecurity. The several slips of the tongue in the play suggest that O'Neill was aware of its Freudian implication. For example, Darrell says, with reference to Evans' weight and high blood pressure, "It's nothing to hope—I meant, to worry over!" (p. 651).

The characters in *Strange Interlude* illustrate a number of neurotic symptoms that invite a psychoanalytic label and description. Nina's preoccupation with Gordon is clearly an obsession. The persistent guilt-ridden memories of Marsden are a form of compulsive reaction. Both Darrell's scientific research and Marsden's literary career are forms of sublimation. Marsden admits that he has written "Fairy Tales for Grown-ups—about . . . lovers who avoid love in hushed whispers" (p. 657). And he correctly evaluates Darrell's work as a "a pretense" and the Doctor as "a scientific dilettante" (p. 629). Their careers are, in part, a substitute for direct sexual expression and aggression.

And from Jung come such concepts as those of the libido, the collective unconscious, archetypal image, introversion and extroversion: Nina's sexual and maternal drives and her urge toward dominance, emphasized at the end of Act VI when she expresses a triumphant sense of power over her four men, are intended as manifestations of libidinal energy. And when in her pregnant state she repeatedly associates herself with the sea and tide, Nina significantly uses the favorite Jungian symbols for the collective unconscious. Likewise, Nina with her voracious desires is unmistakably projected as something of a personification of the anima, the men in the play representing various aspects of the animus. And Marsden and Evans seem to have been intentionally conceived with Jung's description of the introvert and extrovert in mind.

Oscar Cargill has called *Strange Interlude* "a dramatized textbook of all the neuroses discoverable by psychoanalysis."[6] Whether you choose to make a Jungian or Freudian interpretation of Nina's neurosis, it is all there, and all in the popular, over-simplified terms of the 1920's. Gordon's death is the traumatic shock, implicit in the Jungian Scheme which sets the story in motion. One aspect of this shock for Nina is the sudden and drama-tic frustration of mature sexual expression. When this is thwarted, immature sexual impulses emerge and come into conflict with the more mature superego, and guilt ensues. Nina's blaming herself for not having insisted upon physical union with Gordon and her later giving herself sexually to hospitalized war veterans are di-rected by this masochistic urge. A second attempt at mature ful-fillment of the sexual-maternal drives is aborted when she learns of the hereditary insanity in the Evans family. The series of trau-matic shocks and frustrations magnify the intensity of Nina's needs and produce a neurotic woman of insatiable emotional appe-tite. For a moment she attains all her desires through the posses-sion of the various attentions of four men. Sam Evans, as her hus-band, represents domestic security; Charles Marsden, a kind of father surrogate, is the object of a revived Electra complex; Edmund Darrell symbolizes sexual fulfillment; and Gordon, her son, fulfills the maternal drives. In spite of Nina's wishes, the status quo of the relationships cannot be maintained. Nina escapes the most painful consequences of its disruption and her neurosis through a form of regression. Her childhood subjugation to a father symbol revived, Nina views the trials of her adult life as an inter-lude.

For Freud, her neurosis could be said to have originated in an unresolved childhood impulse for sexual union with her father. Any situation which demanded a similar inhibition or repression of sexual desire would revive the guilt associated with that origi-nal Electra complex. Gordon's death frustrated the natural course of Nina's fulfillment. The guilt which she assigns to her failure to consummate their union before his departure is in part the product of a revived Electra attachment. The antagonism she feels toward her father and the desperate need to move away from him indicate a struggle with the impulse and suggest that this is the basic source of Nina's guilt. Repeated failures to attain psychological equilibrium eventually break down her resistance to the Electra tendencies. And at last Nina turns to Marsden, a

[6]Oscar Cargill, *Intellectual America: Ideas on The March* (New York: Mac-millan, 1941), p. 720.

father surrogate, and regresses into childhood. But these do not begin to exhaust the play's psychoanalytic implication.

The 1928 audience saw *Strange Interlude* as not only a convincing demonstration of psychoanalytic principle but as an explication of their own individual and collective psychologies. Historically, it was O'Neill's version of psychoanalysis—and that of other popularizers—rather than Freud's or Jung's which exerted the most significant social influence in the 1920's and beyond.

The theological and ethical controversy explored in *Strange Interlude* reflects that of the period. Largely the story of human beings who had lost faith in traditional morality but who could not escape its influence, *Strange Interlude* is an elaborate conflict between two theologies, the Puritan and Primitive, and two ethical systems, the absolute and relative. Indeed, there are in the play three forces at work and three distinct conceptions of a deity. Corresponding to these three, Nina speaks of wanting "to believe in God at any price—a heap of stones, a snake, a baboon . . . a good man preaching the simple platitudes of truth, those gospel words we love the sound of but whose meaning we pass on to spooks to live by! . . . the modern science God" (p. 523). But science is never in serious contention as an adequate sanction in human life. While Darrell, with his scientific perspective, is conscious of the elemental motivating forces in life and the consequent irrationality of a strict morality, this knowledge enables him neither to accept the Primitive view, that "life is something in one cell that doesn't need to think" (p. 651), nor entirely dispense with the "irrelevant moral ideas" (p. 569) of Puritanism.

The Puritan God is conceived in a male image. Professor Leeds and later Marsden, a father surrogate, represent this deity for Nina. For O'Neill, also, and for many intellectuals during the 1920's, "God the Father" ceased to be a personal deity and became a capricious God for whom "our lives are merely strange dark interludes in the electrical display" (p. 681). Nina finds him "too hard for tired heads and thoroughly comfortless" (p. 525). The absolute and inflexible system of ethical standards related to this Puritan Deity is strongly assailed in *Strange Interlude*. Indeed, as Sophus Winther points out, all the Ten Commandments are violated in one degree or another in the course of the play.[7] What little happiness Nina achieves is, with but few exceptions, through violating traditional standards. By the same rule, most of the suffering in the play is a direct result of either obeying

[7]Sophus Keith Winther, *Eugene O'Neill: A Critical Study* (New York: Harcourt, Brace & Co., 1942), p. 145.

the established Christian code or failing to escape the guilt aroused by a lingering consciousness of that system of morality. It was the "code-bound Gordon" (p. 501) and a Nina held back by the thought of "what would your father say" (p. 502) who failed to consummate their relationship and achieve a degree of happiness. Throughout *Strange Interlude* a sense of guilt and a vision of the death and suffering associated with "God the Father" subvert Nina's happiness: "Black ... in the midst of happiness," she thinks, "black comes ... again ... death ... my father ... comes between me and happiness" (p. 580).

Nina's loss of faith in the Puritan "God the Father" and what he represented led her to a reinterpretation of God based upon a new image, that of a mother. The Primitive God, personified in feminine terms, is associated with the cyclic pattern of life processes. Necessarily amoral, the Primitive nevertheless exerts motivational influences (e.g. Nina's sexual-maternal drives) from which a relativistic or naturalistic ethical philosophy can be derived. *Strange Interlude* is "a play which involves the condemnation of an old ethical theory and the definite implication of a new one to take its place."[8] Actually O'Neill was less than certain about what sort of new ethical system should replace the old. But the play does consider some of the same problems which appear in the controversy between the Modernists, or Liberals and the Fundamentalists in the 1920's. The Modernists, who can be roughly equated with both the Primitive and Scientific-Materialistic forces in the play, were attempting to reconcile the new ideas and norms of social behavior with orthodox theology. Their attempts to more meaningfully define God—as the first cause, as absolute energy, as idealized reality, as a righteous will working in creation, as the ideal and goal toward which all that is highest and best is working—were confusingly varied and ambiguous. Concomitant with the altered concept of the Deity, "practical ethics," a relativistic ethical system based on a standard of general benevolence rather than specific law, became a fashionable theme in the pulpit during the period. O'Neill was, of course, doing much the same in *Strange Interlude*.

With the Modernists attempting to satisfy the skeptic's arguments by reasoning from scientifically demonstrable rather than traditional authority and the Fundamentalists regressing in their theological thinking to the point of rigidly embracing a biblical literalism, the 1920's represented a period of crisis and change both for the church and for individual religious and ethical

[8]*Ibid.,* pp. 138–139.

attitudes—much of the personal dilemma at least reflected in *Strange Interlude*.

"I want you to be happy!" (p. 547); "Be happy, dear! You've got to be happy!" (p. 680)—Mrs. Evans and Nina, the two mothers in *Strange Interlude,* both postulate happiness as a guiding principle for their children. In view of their knowledge of the illusory quality of happiness, the advice seems naive. Mrs. Evans, after a lifetime of sacrifice and fear, incongruously formulates a hedonistic ethical standard characteristic of the 1920's: "Being happy, that's the nearest we can come to knowing what's good . . . the rest is just talk!" (p. 546). Nina's "I shall be happy! (p. 571) becomes in the end "I'm sick of the fight for happiness!" (p. 691). The progression from one to the other exposes happiness as largely an illusion: always elusive, often paid for by the sacrifice of someone else.

The confident prosperity of the decade, the increased leisure and mobility, the greater urge toward self-expression, the high value placed on anything connotative of youth, the reaction to wartime privations, and the contact with Continental versions of the gay life combined to create in the decade a taste for those experiences which brought a direct sense of pleasure rather than those pursuits which created a more permanent, if less immediate, sense of accomplishment. The period was not without real social and cultural progress, but there was an inordinate tendency to "follow the crowd, take up the new toys that were amusing the crowd, go in for the new fads, and savor the amusing scandals and trivialities of life."[9] Among many intellectuals the hedonistic spirit of the 1920's took on an almost belligerent quality. Speaking for people like Ernest Hemingway, F. Scott Fitzgerald, and Edna St. Vincent Millay as well as for himself, Malcom Cowley wrote:

> It is stupid to pile up treasures that we can enjoy only in old age, when we have lost the capacity for enjoyment. Better to seize the moment as it comes, to dwell in it intensely, even at the cost of future suffering. Better to live extravagantly, gather June rose-buds, "burn our candle at both ends."[10]

Darrell, who advises in *Strange Interlude,* "we must all be crooks where happiness is concerned" (p. 493) and "happiness hates the timid" (p. 568) had no more success than his

[9]Frederick Lewis Allen, *The Big Change* (New York: Harper and Bros., 1931), p. 77.
[10]Malcolm Cowley, *Exiles Return* (New York: The Viking Press, 1951), p. 60.

generation—whose shallow and irresponsible chase after happiness may have helped bring on a depression and a war lasting, together, from 1929 to 1945.

Disgusted with the heroic image of Gordan Shaw which infects the lives of everyone in *Strange Interlude,* Darrell condemns but cannot himself escape its influence: "Romantic imagination! It has ruined more lives than all the diseases! Other diseases, I should say! It's a form of insanity" (p. 587). Gordon Shaw is dead before the play begins. The circumstances of his death (as a war hero "brought down in flames . . . two days before the Armistice," p. 487), the nature of his personality ("Gordon's proud spot, fairness and honor!", p. 492), and "his good looks and prowess in sport" (p. 491) prepare the way for his strange deification. To be sure, the hero worship is largely a product of Nina's frustration, but perhaps the age was no less neurotic. While her illusion may or may not be destroyed through emotional exhaustion and age, much of the original image is parodied in her son. Gordon Evans, the living counterpart of the legend, embodies the American concept of perfection in young manhood. Possessing all the extolled virtues and skills, he nevertheless remains empty, spiritless, and dull. In *Strange Interlude,* O'Neill is questioning not only the status of the hero but also the standards by which society judges one.

Nina's deification of Gordon Shaw was paralleled during the 1920's by a national tendency to create public heroes. The inordinate degree of attention they received and the unusual factors influencing their selection were the result of various circumstances. The rise of mass communication (radio, chain newspapers, news services) and mass entertainment (movies, professional and collegiate athletics, antics of exhibitionists), both of which facilitate the creation of heroes, is especially associated with the 1920's. The successful tabloids of the period discovered a phenomenon which eventually became a widespread practice for all forms of public communication and entertainment. By concentrating coverage upon a specific person or incident, a sense of identification was established which stimulated greater public interest. Flagpole sitters, screen stars, marathon dancers, athletes became public heroes. It did not occur to many that the Lindbergh feat was simply a long airplane flight by a capable young man or that Floyd Collins was simply unlucky to have been trapped in that cave.

The spiritual starvation of the American people had created a situation in which hero worship was rampant and irrational. These national heroes, aside from being symptoms of an historical condition, became images which influenced very basically the values of the society. O'Neill apparently recognized all this, for *Strange Interlude* is a critical appraisal of both hero worship and the heroic image of the 1920's. And, as Oscar Cargill so aptly put it, "The skill with which O'Neill brings home the fact that Gordon Shaw, despite his athletic prowess and Apollonian features, must have been a good deal of a wooden image is immeasurably satisfying to one who is tired of handsome football heroes and war heroes and is looking for deeper riches of character."[11]

The business of America in the 1920's was business. The national activity is represented in *Strange Interlude* by Sam Evans, an "overgrown boy" (p. 511) engaged in the "advertising game" (p. 602). Evans, like the pre-depression businessman, does succeed, acquiring all the symbols of a business triumph. O'Neill's apparent attitude is that while business success is at least for the lucky few attainable, the form success takes is itself an illusion. Furthermore, business success as the supreme social ideal has a quite perverse effect upon other professional commitments. Darrell and Marsden, made wealthy through backing Evans, are forced to redefine their life's work as hobbies, emphasizing the subordinate position of creative and scholarly activities to that of business.

Evans, with his superficiality and jovial arrogance, is a caricature rather than a character, suggesting the depersonalizing effect of the business ideal. In *Strange Interlude,* O'Neill is concerned not so directly with the social and cultural values of the system as he is with its influence upon human personality. Sam Evans, the business man, is the only one of the three major male characters who completely "succeeds" and who never questions the validity of his ideals. Although O'Neill apparently intended to thereby demonstrate more effectively the illusory quality of those ideals, Evans' success is an equally satisfactory conclusion in terms of the climate of the period, with its almost mystical attitude toward prosperity in the business world. "Business," in short, "was the typical and preferred activity of the United States, an activity so deeprooted and all embracing that it had become almost a synonym for life itself. Indeed, the struggle for existence, once biological in import, now referred almost exclusively to the battle for survival in the business world."[12] In *Strange Interlude,* Sam Evans embodies a number of illusions

[11]Cargill, *Intellectual America,* p. 707.
[12]Henry M. Robinson, *Fantastic Interim* (New York: Harcourt Brace & Co., 1943), p. 15.

characteristic of a decade monopolized by the business ideal: he accepted the success myth absolutely, even though the Horatio Alger tradition of unlimited personal opportunity was rapidly fading because of technological expansion, subsequent consolidation of business and industry on all levels, and concentration of wealth in the hands of a few. His was an utterly materialistic faith belonging to that pre-1929 era of Florida real-estate and Bull Market booms. And, significantly, as an advertising man he was a part of that modern, mirage creating business based upon lavish display and the manipulation of social values that originated in the 1920's.

Dr. Darrell, the experimental physician, is described in the stage directions of *Strange Interlude* as a kind of prototype of the scientist: "his manners cool and observant, his dark eyes analytical. He has come to consider himself as immune to love through his scientific understanding of its real sexual nature" (p. 515). Ultimately both love and sexual frustration combine to destroy Darrell's illusion and to demonstrate the vulnerability of scientific rationality as a personal philosophy. Darrell eventually denies the creed of the rationalist in his conclusion that "thinking doesn't matter a damn! Life is something in one cell that doesn't need to think!" (p. 651).

Early in the play Darrell prescribed marriage and children as a remedy for Nina's neurosis. An unforeseen factor, the hereditary insanity in her husband's family, interferes. This initial failure of science to solve a human problem demonstrates a flaw in the method; scientific planning requires that all factors operative in any situation be known, and in the area of human affairs this is rarely possible. Darrell, romantically attracted to Nina and at the same time feeling himself at fault because of the failure of his advice, is an eager accomplice when Nina suggests that she have a child by a eugenically sound father. He urges the plan of action in a scene which stands as a parody of the scientific attitude: "In full possession of the facts" and "in the interest of Science" (p. 567, and note the capitalization), Darrell and Nina decide to mate like "guinea pigs" (p. 568).

O'Neill's apparent view that science is largely invalid as a personal and social guide is not incompatible with his acceptance of the psychoanalytic concept of personality. Psychoanalysis, like art, is intuitively derived; Science, generally, is rational. O'Neill's position (and that of many artists) is not easy to explain. He apparently accepts the deterministic principle basic to all scientific thought. (The cause and effect pattern in *Strange Interlude* is emphasized to an almost awkward extreme.) But he denies, perhaps in reaction to popular belief, that science would eventually create the millennium and that in the interim it could comprehend and prescribe cures for all of man's psychological, social, and spiritual ailments.

The invasion of the public mind by scientific ideas in the 1920's was historically unprecedented. Reacting with awe, enthusiasm, and suspicion, people suddenly became conscious of the accumulated theory and fact of the past half century (e.g. the Darwinian theory and planetesimal hypothesis). The word "science" became a shibboleth and the phrase, "science teaches us," as a prefatory statement, silenced all argument. Although a similar credibility of science persists, the decade of the 20's was unique for its unquestioning reliability upon any proposition which bore a scientific label.

The status of science was the result of various circumstances. The latter part of the 19th and the early 20th centuries were a time of impressive progress in applied and theoretical science. The First World War served as an impetus for both science and industry. A marriage of the two introduced the public to numerous products which suddenly revolutionized their living patterns. It was for example, during the 1920's that the automobile became a common possession. But the monotony of the assembly line, growing competition between men and machines, unsettling social and philosophical effects of such "scientifically" derived ideas as Economic Darwinism, and the natural ebb which follows every excess of enthusiasm combined to create a new impression. The utopian view of science predominant at the opening of the decade gave way toward the end to a growing sense of disillusionment. And Eugene O'Neill's *Strange Interlude* is a revealing study of this shift in public opinion.

Charles Marsden's confession—

> All the twenty odd books I've written have been long winded fairy tales for grown-ups—about dear old ladies and witty, cynical bachelors and quaint characters with dialects, and married folk who always admire and respect each other, and lovers who avoid love in hushed whispers! That's what I've been, Nina—a hush-hush whisperer of lies! (pp. 657–658)

—is another allusion to a much discussed subject of the 1920's— artistic integrity. Marsden, instead of revealing life through his novels, escapes it. He says of himself, "I've never married the word to life!" (p. 624). Darrell is Marsden's most penetrating

critic. (The natural philosophic enmity between the rational scientist and the intuitive artist is explored by O'Neill as a means for
dramatically analyzing their mutual illusions.) His description of
Marsden is probably accurate: "his novels just well-written surface . . . no depth, no digging underneath . . . afraid he'll meet
himself somewhere . . . one of those poor devils who spend their
lives trying not to discover what sex they belong to!" (p. 516).
Clearly Marsden represents that stream of literature characterized by reticence, optimism, and traditional form, while the
pattern emerging during the 1920's was marked by its frankness,
pessimism (or at least realism), and experimental form. O'Neill,
with his naturalistic dialogue, penetrating study of human desires
and frustrations, tendency toward negation, and restless experimenting, probably shared many of the literary values of novelists
like Ernest Hemingway, Theodore Dreiser, Thomas Wolfe, and
John Dos Passos. But the same factors which stimulated a literary
renaissance during a decade obsessed with self-expression also
created a climate favorable for the dilettante. And *Strange Interlude* is an appeal for greater integrity in literature and literary
taste.

   Strange Interlude is, of course, art—not history. But its
themes—psychoanalysis, theological and ethical controversy,
hedonism, hero worship, business, science, and art—are distinctly those of America in the 1920's; and its characters and
situations are reminiscent of the decade. Though it has lost some
of its appeal as literature, Eugene O'Neill's *Strange Interlude*
retains an unsurpassing attraction for any reader interested in that
most inaccessible of historical periods—the recent past.

John H. Raleigh

Mourning Becomes Electra *and* A Touch of the Poet

The two most comprehensive O'Neill plays about the New England nineteenth century are *Mourning Becomes Electra* and *A Touch of the Poet*. As history, they are complementary, and contrasting, accounts of similar historical events: the decay of the Anglo-Puritan aristocracy (treated in both plays); and the emergence of the Irish-Catholic underdogs *(A Touch of the Poet)*.

In *Mourning Becomes Electra* the sinister, scarlet sunset is ubiquitous. The first scene of the first act of the first play, *Homecoming,* opens in the afterglow of a sunset, with the white porticos of the Mannon temple bathed in a "crimson" light. This is to be the chief "light" of the trilogy. This recurring crimson sky, always steadily deepening, in *Mourning Becomes Electra* signifies one thing: death. Underneath the play's Freudianism; its analogizing to Greek myth; its recurrent incest motif, generation after generation; its contrast between the uninhibited sexuality of the South Seas and the rigid prudery of New England and the accompanying contrast between the freedom, rhythm, brightness, and beauty of life at sea and the restrictions, mechanization, darkness, and dreariness of life on land; underneath all these devices and themes is the ubiquity of death. This is not only a question of the two murders (those of Ezra Mannon and Adam Brant) and the two suicides (Christine Mannon and Orin Mannon), but of the very fabric of the thought of the play, wherein the characters are not only trapped by their own dead but are also continually, tortuously meditating upon death. No one ever reaches a conclusion; all they know, with any certainty, is that death is surely, inexorably devouring the Mannons, their power, and their way of life. In Act III of *Homecoming* the newly returned Ezra Mannon, home from the war, cannot stop talking about death, despite his wife's pleas that he cease: "That's al-

From The Plays of Eugene O'Neill *by John H. Raleigh. Southern Illinois University Press, 1965. Reprinted by permission.*

ways been the Mannons' way of thinking. They went to the white meetinghouse on Sabbaths and meditated on death. Life was a dying. Being born was starting to die. Death was being born." But the war, seeing too many white walls splattered with blood "that counted no more than dirty water," made all this seem meaningless, "so much solemn fuss over death!" Real death has taught him the meaninglessness of imagined death, the Mannon obsession. But by dawn he will be death's victim, murdered by his wife. Ironically, he had earlier observed to his wife: "All victory ends in the defeat of death." But he does not know if defeats "end in the victory of death."

Death symbols and themes are woven into the play in all kinds of ways. For example, the ancestral Mannons, whose portraits glare down from the walls of the house, were "witch-burners." Again, the black-white symbolism that is endemic in O'Neill's plays, and in American literature generally, is pervasive in *Mourning Becomes Electra:* the white faces set off by black clothing; the white porticos of the house dimming into darkness; and so on. And as in Melville, white does not signify purity; rather it means the charnel house. The sound effects concur. The first song heard is "John Brown's Body." The theme song of the play, "Shenandoah," is meant to signify the more somber aspects of the sea *("a song that more than any other holds in it the brooding rhythm of the sea").* The drunken chanty-man of Act IV of *The Hunted* staggers off singing "Hanging Johnny." Even American history plays a role in generating this aura of the charnel house, for the seminal national events in the background of the play are the Civil War, the greatest carnage experienced on American soil, and the assassination of Lincoln, its greatest single political tragedy. Moreover, beautiful, rhythmic ways of life are dying too, with the clipper giving way to the steamer. As the chantyman drunkenly and lugubriously laments to Adam Brant, the owner of a beautiful clipper: "Aye, but it ain't fur long, steam is comin' in, the sea is full of smoky tea-kettles, the old days is dyin', and where'll you an' me be then? *(Lugubriously drunken again)* Everything is dyin'! Abe Lincoln is dead."

Mourning Becomes Electra is not only O'Neill's "death" play; it is also, and logically, his "war" play. The Civil War is, of course, the chief agent in the plot, for it is Ezra and Orin's absence in the war that allows the conditions for the tragedy to emerge.

O'Neill on several previous occasions had dealt with that other great contrast in which mankind seems to be permanently involved, war and peace. An early one-acter, *The Sniper,* is a not very skillful anti-war propaganda tract. And the naturally corrupt Benny of *Diff'rent* had been even further corrupted by reason of having been in the American Expeditionary Force in World War I (safely behind the lines). Nina of *Strange Interlude* had lost her Gordon in World War I. But it is in *Mourning Becomes Electra* that O'Neill treats of war most extensively and somberly. If peace, in O'Neill's world, is hell, war is worse. On battle itself O'Neill was of Tolstoi's school: individual engagements are a series of accidents whose only meaning is the irony of human affairs. Orin, who is the spokesman for the hatred of war, blunders in war and becomes, naturally and logically, a hero. In Act III of *The Hunted* he explains how it happened. He had been in the trenches at Petersburg, had not been able to sleep, and felt "queer" in the head. Like a good soldier, he thought that generals were stupid and he wished that the soldiers on both sides would suddenly throw down their weapons, shake hands, and laugh. So he did, in fact, begin to laugh and walk toward the Southern lines with his hand out. What he got for his pains was a wound in the head, which drove him temporarily mad. He ran on yelling, wanting to kill somebody. This excited a lot of "our fools" and they went crazy too, following Orin and capturing a part of the Southern line they had not dared tackle before. He had acted in all this without orders, but his father, the General, decided it would be better to overlook this and let his son be a hero. "So do you wonder I laugh!" But by and large war is not a joke, and the war itself is never over, "Not inside us who killed!" (*The Hunted,* III). Still, the Civil War became the Mannons. In Orin's words, as he surveys the dead body of his unlamented father: "Who are you? Another corpse! You and I have seen fields and hillsides sown with them—and they meant nothing!—nothing but a dirty joke life plays on life! *(Then with a dry smile)* Death sits so naturally on you! Death becomes the Mannons!" *(ibid.).* Significantly, the only positive Mannon accomplishment in the war was negative. Grant had nicknamed Ezra Mannon "Old Stick," an abbreviation for "Stick-in-the-Mud," for while General Mannon was worth nothing on offense, he could hold ground forever, "until hell froze over!" *(ibid.).*

In a queer, complicated Mannon way the killing of others is in reality a form of self-destruction. Orin says in Act III of *The Hunted* that in the war he had the "queer" feeling that he was murdering the same man over and over again and that he would discover in the end that the man was really himself. After he kills Brant, his mother's lover, and notices Brant's Mannon countenance, a masklike look that always appears to be fighting life, he exclaims on the resemblance of Brant to his father and to that "man" that he had killed over and over again in the war. The man's face had a habit of changing into that of his father and finally of himself, and in killing Brant he thinks that maybe he has "committed suicide."

This is the real meaning of the trilogy considered as an historical document: the Puritan aristocracy willing its own destruction. And one does not in this world have to have been in the war to be obsessed with and dominated by death. The very mansion is infected by the taint of mortality. As Seth, the hired hand, says in the first scene of *The Haunted:* "There's been evil in that house since it was first built in hate—and it's kept growin' there ever since, as what's happened there has proved." There is in the trilogy the usual hint, in the imagination of a woman, that some kind of evil and implacable deity is behind it all. This notion—the Mary Tyrone speech—is given to Christine Mannon in Act I of *The Haunted* in a dialogue with Hazel, the "nice" young lady of the play. Christine too had once been innocent and loving and trusting, like Hazel, but "God won't leave us alone"; He tortures and wrings and twists human lives with "others' lives until—we poison each other to death!" But, as in most of O'Neill's tragedies, no exact balance is ever struck between fate and free will. And the men, on their part, think, simply, that a Mannon is a Mannon and this signifies death. Thus Orin sets out to write a history of the Mannon family in order to trace out to its secret hiding place the evil destiny that has dominated the Mannon family. He finds no answer and can only make the observation to Lavinia that he finds her the "most interesting criminal" of them all. And he concludes too that the Mannons are not special in any way but are only mankind writ large. He thus takes himself, prematurely aged, guilt-ridden, sitting in a dark room and writing about sin and death by a dim lamp, to be a symbol of man's fate—"a lamp burning out in a room of waiting shadows!" (*The Haunted,* II).

Furthermore, where death's dominion leaves off, there begin the tortures of guilt. In Orin's words: "The only love I can know now is the love of guilt for guilt which breeds more guilt—until you get so deep at the bottom of hell there is no lower you can sink and you rest there in peace!" (*ibid.*, III). Ironically, the last Mannon, Lavinia, is not given the blessed relief of death but is doomed, instead, to a continued existence of death-in-life: "I'm not asking God or anybody for forgiveness. I forgive myself!

(She leans back and closes her eyes again—bitterly) I hope there is a hell for the good somewhere!" "Love isn't permitted to me. The dead are too strong!" "I'm the last Mannon. I've got to punish myself!" "It takes the Mannons to punish themselves for being born!" *(ibid.,* IV). These mortal sentiments of Lavinia bring the thought of the play back full circle to her father's original remarks on the Mannon preoccupation with death. She then withdraws into the mansion, which will be boarded up, with a *"strange cruel smile of gloating"* over the coming years of self-torture.

The pendant and companion piece to *Mourning Becomes Electra* is *A Touch of the Poet,* which is once more about the incipient decline of an aristocratic New England family. But it differs radically from *Mourning Becomes Electra* in two important respects: it shows the beginnings of the social climb of the Irish Catholics, and the overall theme of the play is not death but its opposite, love. So while the dramatic movement of *Mourning Becomes Electra* is a narrowing and constricting, back to death and extinction, the total movement—despite Con Melody's tragedy—of the dramatic action of *A Touch of the Poet* is a broadening out and a leap forward, as Sara Melody makes the jump into an aristocratic New England family, from which union will follow, in effect, a new race, the Anglo-Irish, just as the end of *The Haunted* signifies the end of a Yankee genetic strain. This is not a question of personal happiness, and in *More Stately Mansions,* which shows Sara married, this particular Cinderella does not live happily ever after. Rather it is initial release of a pent-up race and culture. To underline the theme of Yankee decline, O'Neill chose as his historical background for *A Touch of the Poet* the 1828 presidential contest between Andrew Jackson and John Quincy Adams, by which a "common man" became President, and the Adams family, *the* New England aristocratic family, was ushered off the national scene, even though John Quincy Adams was to return to Washington as a congressman.

In most respects these two New England plays are diametric opposites. As *Mourning Becomes Electra* is about, among other things, female destructiveness, *A Touch of the Poet* is in part about female creativity, the somewhat Barryesque notion that romantic love is not only woman's creation but does not even depend on its supposed source and object, the beloved male. Men, so the play implies, are all for pursuing ideas or forms to some inhuman extreme and for knocking heads together and trying to kill one another in the name of their impossible pride, but

women, like "God's glue," hold it all together, whatever the men
may think is happening. In the last act of the play Sara makes the
discovery, after her successful and satisfying seduction of Simon
Harford, that her mother's undying love for her impossible husband, Con, is not folly, as she had thought, but wisdom: "Sure,
I've always known you're the sweetest woman in the world,
Mother, but I never suspected you were a wise woman too, until
I knew tonight the truth of what you said this morning, that a
woman can forgive whatever the man she loves could do and still
love him, because it was through him she found the love in herself; that, in one way, he doesn't count at all, because it's love,
your own love, your love in him, and to keep that your pride will
do anything" (IV). Men would be shamed, in their boasting and
vanity, if they but knew that women are not the slaves of men but
the slaves of love itself. If a woman, Lavinia, is the worst criminal
of all in *Mourning Becomes Electra,* a woman, Nora, is the best
person in *A Touch of the Poet.* In Act I she is described as
lovable, simple, sweet, charming, and dauntless, with a never-
quenched spirit.

   If the memories of the Civil War that play so important a role
in *Mourning Becomes Electra* are to the effect that "war is hell,"
the war memories of the Napoleonic era that operate in the
background of *A Touch of the Poet* imply that battle is a glorious
thing: brilliant uniforms, cavalry charges, heroism, and glory.[1]
Only his memories of his triumphs at the battle of Talavera, in
Wellington's Peninsular Campaign, and his splendid officer's
uniform, barely sustain the character of Con Melody throughout
most of the play, whereas in *Mourning Becomes Electra* Orin
Mannon's war memories are only another aspect of his obsession
with, and descent to, death.

---

   [1]Historically, of course, the Napoleonic era saw the last of the "romantic"
wars, while the American Civil War was the first modern conflict.

Elder Olson

Modern Drama and Tragedy:
A View of Mourning Becomes Electra

Do we have tragedy in modern times? If so, of what sort is it? If not, why not? And what difference does it make?

The best way to answer these questions is consider some specimens. *Mourning Becomes Electra* strikes me as excellent for our purposes, for a number of reasons. It is often called O'Neill's supreme achievement; O'Neill himself has the reputation of being among the most serious of modern dramatists—indeed, he is often spoken of as America's first real tragic dramatist; and he founded his trilogy upon the legends which underlie the *Oresteia*.

I suppose that nobody of any sense goes around with complete summaries of plots in his head; so it will be well to recall what happens in *Mourning Becomes Electra*. We had better recall O'Neill's purpose first: he was trying to write a modern psychological drama, with some approximation to the Greek sense of fate, so that an audience which no longer believed in gods or supernatural retribution might still have something like that sense, and be moved accordingly. For a number of very good reasons which we need not go into, he set his trilogy in New England. The Trojan War became the Civil War. He gave his characters names somewhat resembling those of their Greek prototypes: Agamemnon became Asa Mannon, ultimately Ezra Mannon; Clytemnestra became Christine; Electra became Eleanor, Ellen, Elsa, Laodicea, and finally Lavinia; Orestes became Orin, and Aegisthus became Adam.

O'Neill had more in mind than a modernization of the Greeks; he was also trying to remedy what he took to be a deficiency in Greek drama. Electra, he felt, had been allowed to "peter out . . . into married life," as he puts it. Why was there no Greek play about her after the death of Clytemnestra? Why should she be exempt from retribution? Pursuit of these questions

From Elder Olson, Tragedy and the Theory of Drama, *1961. Copyright © 1961 by the Wayne State University Press. Reprinted by permission.*

led him to make her the central figure of his drama, and the emphasis is reflected in the title.

Homecoming, The Hunted, and *The Haunted* make up the three plays of *Mourning Becomes Electra.* In *Homecoming,* Christine, who has been having a liaison with Adam Brant, awaits the return of her husband from the war. Lavinia, herself secretly in love with Adam, has discovered the liaison and tells her mother that it must be broken off. Christine plots with Adam to poison Ezra. On the morning after his homecoming Ezra and Christine quarrel, Ezra has a heart attack, and Christine gives him poison instead of his heart medicine. Lavinia discovers the poison bottle, surmises what has happened, and determines on revenge.

In *The Hunted* Orin returns. Always greatly attached to his mother, he grows jealous of Adam. Under Lavinia's urgings his feelings grow more violent; ultimately, having tracked Christine to Adam's ship and discovered their rendezvous, he shoots Adam after his mother has departed. The murder is taken to be the deed of ship-robbers; but Lavinia and Orin disclose the truth to Christine, as well as their knowledge of her guilt. Christine commits suicide.

In *The Haunted* Lavinia, who has come to resemble her mother more and more, becomes the object of Orin's strange affection. Orin ultimately recognizes this as incestuous desire for both her and his mother. He proposes incestuous relations to Lavinia. When she rejects him in horror, he kills himself. Lavinia herself at last realizes that her attachment to her fiancé is nothing but her desire for the dead Adam; she frightens off her lover and gives herself over to a life as a recluse, to suffer the tortures of remorse until her death.

This brief summary does more than the usual injustice done by such things, but perhaps it will serve our purposes. O'Neill has the Greeks in mind, is even vying with them, and invites comparison with them. Well, then: how does *Mourning Becomes Electra* compare with the *Oresteia*?

Atreus and Thyestes are here represented by two persons outside the play, Grandfather Abe Mannon and his brother David. There is no banquet; simply, both brothers are in love with the same woman, Marie Brantôme (Aerope as a Canuck nurse-girl); and when David wins her, Abe in revenge cheats David out of his share of the estate, and the lovers, along with their son Adam, suffer extreme poverty. David is a drunkard and weakling; when Adam grows up, he comes to detest the very name of Mannon and adopts his mother's name in the shortened version of Brant. He enters into the play, thus, quasi-incognito. He seduces Christine in vengeance against the Mannons but falls in love with her. He agrees to help in the murder of Ezra—his help consists in procuring the poison—partly because he wants Christine, partly because he wants revenge against Ezra, partly because he wants a ship.

Even this much suggests a general debasement of character, motive, and action; and further examination establishes it beyond doubt. What is the difference between Clytemnestra and Christine, Agamemnon and Ezra Mannon, Electra and Lavinia, Orestes and Orin? The Aeschylean figures are all of an imposing stature; O'Neill's are not. As against the superb and "manly-minded" Clytemnestra, Christine is weak, cowardly, irresolute, spiteful, and wholly the puppet of her emotions and desires. Clytemnestra kills out of a whole complex of powerful motives, as we know; Christine kills because Ezra disgusts her and Adam attracts her. Clytemnestra *must* kill; I have never been convinced that Christine has sufficient reason to. Clytemnestra commits a violent and daring murder, and makes a bold and triumphant avowal of it. Christine treacherously poisons a sick man, already helpless in a paroxysm, and seeks to conceal her crime. We do not approve of Clytemnestra's crime, but we are compelled to respect her in the doing of it; we have the sense that horrible as her deed is, she thinks of it in some strange way as just and right. But it is impossible to have any respect whatsoever for Christine. In the whole history of literature we find no other woman who can match—in her special way—the Clytemnestra of Aeschylus; not even Lady Macbeth. But we have met Christines in countless melodramas, and the police courts find her a very familiar figure indeed.

Orin and Lavinia are similarly debasements of their prototypes. Orestes commits actual matricide, in horror and revulsion, under divine direction; Orin is a psychotic, moved by unconscious incestuous desires; and his guilt in his mother's death is merely fancied. Electra suffers dishonor, privation, and oppression, sees her people laboring under tyranny, and her father's murderers flourishing unpunished; she acts to restore justice. Lavinia is a girl cheated of her love by her mother. True, O'Neill penetrates the moral pretexts of his characters, to reveal them as merely animal drives; but that penetration is itself a debasement. One cannot dignify human beings by regarding them as animals.

Suppose, then, that there are these debasements. What does it matter?

It matters a very great deal, so far as the seriousness of the action is concerned. O'Neill supposed that the seriousness of Greek tragedy depended upon belief in the gods, in divine intervention and retribution. He was completely mistaken. We regard as serious whatever can importantly affect our happiness or misery; whatever can give great pleasure or pain, mental or physical; whatever similarly affects the happiness or pleasure of those for whom we have some concern, or of a good number of people, or of people whom we take to be of considerable worth; or whatever involves a principle upon which all such things depend; or anything that bears a sufficient resemblance to these, or a sufficient relation. In the *Agamemnon* . . . every one of these elements of seriousness was involved in the action and . . . the poet used every device to give us the *sense* of their importance. It is that sense of tremendous importance which is effective, not the theology; and the proof of this is that "an intelligent audience of today, possessed of no belief in gods or supernatural retribution"—I am quoting O'Neill's description of the audience he thought he was addressing—is still profoundly moved by the Aeschylean drama.

And consequently the substitution of believed Freudian doctrines for unbelieved theology will not work. Such beliefs can have no great emotive force in themselves. They can affect us only as they relate to things which do have such force, to things which already embody the values of which I have been speaking. An animal drive or impulse, no matter how firmly we are convinced of its existence, can only affect us through our reflection on its capacity to produce goods and evils of a certain nature, magnitude, and duration.

O'Neill's trilogy, thus, can have only limited seriousness. The misfortunes are confined to a single family, affecting the fate of no one outside it. They are not conceived as involving any principle upon which the happiness of all of us or most of us must depend. They do not even *resemble* anything likely to happen to any great number of us. And they do not happen to persons whom we value highly. They can only affect us as they play upon our philanthropic feelings; and O'Neill, in so limited a dramatic conception, can only move us by insisting upon the intensity of the suffering of his characters. I am not at all sure that he himself knows *what* they feel; certainly we do not; perhaps all that anyone knows is that the Mannons are having a rather bad time.

I must conclude, therefore, that if tragedy displays an action of the utmost seriousness and significance, *Mourning Becomes Electra* is not a tragedy. I am not saying that it should have been tragedy or even that I am sorry it is not tragedy. I am simply saying that it is not. Yet, as I said earlier, a work seems always to make a proposal. I cannot avoid the feeling here that O'Neill somehow proposed something of tragic quality and that he failed because he failed to comprehend what was supremely serious and significant.

Travis Bogard

The Iceman Cometh

O'Neill wrote the first draft of *The Iceman Cometh* between June 8 and November 26, 1939. In this year, the world fell apart as Poland was invaded and Britain and France declared war on Germany. Throughout the end of the Depression, O'Neill had worked on the cycle, finishing drafts of *And Give Me Death*, *The Greed of the Meek* and *More Stately Mansions*. Work on *The Calms of Capricorn* had begun, but the world crisis made it impossible for him to continue his account of the decline and fall of the United States. In the midst of Armageddon, one does not bother to prophesy. O'Neill's reaction to war was predictable. At Tao House, he retreated further into himself than he had ever gone before, as if the only understanding that could come in a world gone mad was the understanding of one's self. The following year he wrote *Hughie* and the scenarios and some draft versions of its companion works in the cycle of one-act plays called *By Way of Obit*. In 1941, he wrote his last completed work, *A Moon for the Misbegotten*. Although he picked at the cycle, making revisions on *A Touch of the Poet* as late as 1942, the work was at a stalemate. Whatever truths it contained for O'Neill had finally to be explored in another past, his own, and in another way than he had in the cycle. The last four plays form a network of introspection whose effect is perhaps best expressed in O'Neill's words about *The Iceman Cometh* contained in a letter to Lawrence Langner dated August 11, 1940:

> . . . there are moments in it that suddenly strip the secret soul of a man stark naked, not in cruelty or moral superiority, but with an understanding compassion which sees him as a victim of the ironies of life and of himself. Those moments are for me the depth of tragedy, with nothing more than can possibly be said.

Compassion produced by a full understanding of man's circumstances and man's essential nature, a compassion which beggars analysis, is O'Neill's final achievement in theater. The action of each of the four last plays rests in a tale to be told, a tale that is essentially a confession made in hope of absolution. Although the confessional tale is often plotless, often nothing more than a dream, it is a way of reaching out in the dark, of finding pity long denied to old sorrow.

The introspective qualities of the last plays account for their essential lyricism. When *The Iceman Cometh* was first produced in 1946, under the somewhat ponderously reverential conditions that O'Neill's "return" to the New York theater necessarily occasioned, it brought with it, from producers and reviewers, charges that O'Neill was indulging himself by refusing to cut the work. Langner tells of a time during rehearsals when he timidly reminded O'Neill that the same point had been made eighteen times. O'Neill told him "in a particularly quiet voice, 'I *intended* it to be repeated eighteen times!' " Although it was obviously not a matter of calculated intention, O'Neill did not indulge in such repetition without full awareness of its theatrical consequences. Like many of his earlier efforts, the repetition not only in *The Iceman Cometh* but in *A Long Day's Journey into Night* is essential to the lyric mode of the work, for in these plays O'Neill became the poet he had earlier so often lamented he could not be.

Perhaps the nearest theatrical analogue to *The Iceman Cometh* is Dylan Thomas's *Under Milkwood*. Both are "plays for voices," and the voices are those of the dead, reiterating their stories endlessly in an eternity of silence. Under the circumstances of the play the period slang takes on the special qualities of lyric speech.[1] The movement is musical; the repetition of what is said, often almost without significant development, must be followed as if it were music, as patterned abstraction, implemented through contrapuntal repetitions. It is a kind of "sound effect," but here blended so completely with the action that it becomes the action. There are not many moments in theater comparable to the canonical weaving of the narratives of betrayal, Hickey's and Parritt's, toward the end of the play. Hickey's long monologue is interspersed by short echoing comments from Parritt telling Larry Slade of his own act of betrayal. Parritt and Hickey do not, really, listen to the words that are said. That is to say they do not understand one another and from that understanding receive direction. Rather, they move toward the same

---

[1] O'Neill has taken care to make the speech of his characters accurate. Cf. for example, *Hugo of* The Iceman Cometh: *Realism and O'Neill*, Doris M. Alexander, *American Quarterly* V (Winter, 1953), 357–66.

end without conscious inter-awareness, impelled by purely verbal concatenations, each developing the theme of betrayal as a sound in the air. *The Iceman Cometh* does not need music, yet it should be heard as music is heard with an understanding that it progresses in patterns of sound, as much as in patterns of narrative action.

To argue that a play should not be justified by comparison to a musical form has validity. It is, after all, only an analogy, but O'Neill's predilection for Nietzsche would cause him to know that Nietzsche claimed tragedy to have been born from "The Spirit of Music." The lyric movement of the chorus in an Aeschylean or Sophoclean tragedy, *The Coephorii* or *Antigone*, for example, is the source of the play's energy, turning as a massive wheel at the center of the narrative, spinning off the tortured action, and giving it life and form. Similarly, *The Iceman Cometh* has a strong choric thrust, developed in lyric repetitions.

The Iceman Cometh is perhaps the most "Greek" of O'Neill's work, built around a central chorus, complete with *choregos* in Harry Hope, and the three principal actors, Hickey, Slade and Parritt. In creating his chorus, O'Neill turned to his memories of time spent in the saloons of lower New York— Jimmy the Priest's, The Hell Hole, the Golden Swan—and of the people he had met there. Most of the characters are modeled after acquaintances or friends he had observed and whom he placed on stage with special fidelity.[2] Yet, while he is concerned to specify their individuality with affectionate concern, he is also seeking, somewhat in the manner of the Elizabethan "Character" writers,

[2] Arthur and Barbara Gelb and Louis Sheaffer have devoted extensive research to the identification of the real-life sources for O'Neill's characters. Of the cast only Rocky, Morello, the three women and, of course, Moran and Liebe, both extras, appear to have no actual counterparts, although even here the possibility is that they are formed from memory. The only significant exception appears to be Hickey. The Gelbs suggest that he was based on a character named "Happy," a collector for a laundry chain whom O'Neill had known in The Hell Hole. An aspect of the portrait was derived from characteristics of Jamie, who, it will be remembered, had appeared in a supporting role in a play called *The Travelling Salesman*. Sheaffer points to a character named Adams in the unpublished *Chris Christophersen*. The play opens with a scene between Adams, Burns and "Johnny the Priest." Adams, like the inhabitants of Hope's saloon is asleep at a table. The action begins with Burns attempting to wake Adams. Johnny, the bartender-owner intervenes:

> JOHNNY   (*Frowning*) Leave him alone, Jack. He's been talking me deaf, dumb and blind all day. I'm sick o' listening to him. Let him sleep it off.
>
> BURNS   You? Huh! How about me? I'm going to make him buy 'nother drink, that's what—to pay me for listenin' to his bull, see?

to see in the individual a type. The word "type" occurs frequently in his descriptive stage directions of Hope's roomers: Hugo Kalmar bears "a strong resemblance to the type of Anarchist is portrayed . . . in newspaper cartoons"; Joe Mott's face is "mildly negroid in type"; Piet Wetjoen is "a Dutch farmer type." Where the word is not mentioned, the idea remains: James Cameron has "a quality about him of a prim, Victorian old maid." Cecil Lewis "is as obviously English as Yorkshire pudding and just as obviously the former army officer." McGloin has "the occupation of policeman stamped all over him." Ed Mosher "looks like an enlarged, elderly, bald edition of the village fat boy." While the typicality of Willie Oban and of the bartender Rocky is not stressed (although Rocky is summarized as a "Neapolitan-American"), they are not essentially different from the other members of the chorus. The same is true of the three women: Pearl and Margie are called "typical dollar streetwalkers," and Chuck Morello, the daytime bartender, like his nighttime counterpart, is seen as an "Italian-American." Harry Hope, the chorus leader, is not viewed as typical in the same way. He maintains a certain individuality partly because it is through him that the liaison is made between the actions of the chorus and the principals. These—Larry Slade, Don Parritt and Theodore Hickman—are individuals, less by their appearance than by the complexity of their emotional problems.

The tableau thus formed, although externally static, has a powerful inner movement. The unity of the chorus is achieved by a remarkable theatrical *tour de force*. Each of the derelicts has, in the Stanislavskian sense, the same essential action: to foster himself in his dream. The actions create the unity of the microcosm O'Neill has woven. Against its fabric, the protagonists stand sharply drawn. Parritt, Slade and Hickey are seen, perhaps, as

---

He wakes Adams, they argue about the purchase of a drink and finally Burns dozes off while Adams sits *"staring at him with sodden stupidity."* He comes to a short while later, becomes noisy and is sent protesting upstairs to bed. When he has gone, Johnny says of him, "Smart fellow, too—when he's sober. I've known him for twenty or thirty years. Used to be a clerk at a ship chandler's. Left that and became a travelling salesman. Good one, too, they say. Never stays long on one job, though. Booze got a strangle hold on him. He's been fired again now. Good schoolin'—every chance, too. He's one of the kind ought to leave red eye alone. Always ending up his drunk here. Knows no one'll know him here 'cept me and he ain't shamed to go the limit. *(Philosophically)* Well, he's a good spender as long as he's got it. Don't be too rough with him."

The detail of the portrait suggests that O'Neill drew it from a model, especially since Adams disappears from the script at this point. Here probably is the unnamed progenitor of Hickey.

aspects of the same man. They overlap at least, in their acts of betrayal, their despairing desire to be rid of pity, their refusal to enter the world of the dreaming chorus. Yet, although they resemble one another, they stand opposed as antagonists as well, forming a hostile triangle against the unity of the background.

The physical picture awakens echoes of other works. O'Neill has evidently had his eye on Gorky's *The Lower Depths,* a play which he appreciated as "the great proletarian revolutionary play," saying that "it is really more wonderful propaganda for the submerged than any other play ever written, simply because it contains no propaganda, but simply shows humanity as it is—truth in terms of human life." The relation between the two works bears analysis, as does the relationship between O'Neill's play and Ibsen's *The Wild Duck,* which like *The Iceman Cometh* explores the fatal effects of the "life-lie." In configuration and *dramatis personae,* Harry Hope's birthday party bears a strong resemblance to the traditional images of "The Last Supper."[3] Such parallels are just and important and in part serve to explain why *The Iceman Cometh* now ranks among the most ambiguous of O'Neill's plays and has received the most extensive critical attention. In its original production, which marked the end of O'Neill's absence from the theater, and in its 1956 revival in New York, a production that began the resurgence of interest in O'Neill's dramas, it has held a special position in the canon.

Yet viewed in its place in the progress of O'Neill's playwriting career it is not an ambiguous work. In part, it stands as an ironic comment on much that had preceded. Reverting to his earlier manner, spinning an all-but-plotless play filled with por-

---

[3] Cf. Cyrus Day, "The Iceman and the Bridegroom," in *Modern Drama,* I, 1, May, 1958, pp. 3–9. Professor Day's article lists a number of resemblances between Hope's party and The Last Supper, including the twelve "disciples" of Hickey, the three women, the presence of Parritt as a suicidal Judas figure, the wine drinking, the midnight hour. Day is in error when he states that the stage grouping resembles Da Vinci's Last Supper. O'Neill throughout the play has been very specific as to where each person sits at the tables. At the party, Hickey and Hope face one another from opposite ends of the table, Larry and Parritt occupy the central positions facing the viewer where Da Vinci places Christ. The point is perhaps unimportant except that it raises the question as to who is the Christ figure at this "supper," Hickey or Harry Hope? Professor Day's view is that Hickey is a form of anti-Christ and that the play is blasphemously nihilistic ("Did [O'Neill] introduce concealed blasphemies into his play ...? And did he laugh in secret at critics who supposed he had written a compassionate play ...?"). The party is, after all, Hope's party, and it is Hope who rises from the death they suffer to bring life again to the bums. O'Neill's compassion in this play, while it may rest on ambiguities, and while it was born of despair, is not fraudulent.

traits of the down-and-out characters he has known as a young
man, he recapituates many of his early themes, particularly that
of the "hopeless hope," but removes the romantic coloration
with which he clothed the concept in *The Straw*, seeing it now as
he was to show it again in *Hughie,* as the only lifeline man could
find.

The title, drawn from the story of the wise and foolish virgins
in Matthew 25:6, parodies the description of the coming of the
Savior: "But at midnight there was a cry made, Behold the
bridegroom cometh." The savior who comes to Harry Hope's
saloon is a strange messiah. The image of the iceman, suggestive
of the chill of the morgue, and of a variety of off-color stories and
songs featuring the iceman as a casual seducer,[4] is interpreted by
Willie Oban as meaning death: "Would that Hickey or Death
would come." Hickey is a messiah of death, but his message,
judged by its effect on its hearers, is closely parallel to that of
O'Neill's other messiah, Lazarus of Bethany.

O'Neill's two choric dramas, both with titles derived from
the New Testament, are at once remarkably like and yet start-
lingly opposite to one another. In both *The Iceman Cometh* and
Lazarus Laughed, a messianic figure appears preaching salvation
to a world represented in microcosm by type characters. In each
play, the recipients of the message prove resistant to it, and when
it is forced upon them, prove incapable of acting in accord with it.
In each, the messiah is set free to follow his own path to martyr-
dom by the murder of his wife. That path leads to burning—at the
stake and in the electric chair. Such parallels are meaningless
except as they relate to the central matter: the messages both
messiahs preach, however different in effect and intention, are in
essence the same. Of *Lazarus Laughed* O'Neill wrote "Death is
the Father, Fear the Holy Spirit, Pain the Son." To this trinity
man pays his homage. Lazarus's message to rid men of fear and
pain is that they should see life as illusory, give over the dreams
that haunt them like ghosts in the dark and acknowledge with
clear eyes that they are part of life itself and can ask no higher

---

[4]Like the traveling salesman, the iceman gained a certain mythic dimension
in American smoking-car jokes. Dudley Nichols recorded that O'Neill had wished
to recall the Biblical quotation by his use of the archaic verb form, but that he also
wanted to suggest the bawdy story of the husband who called upstairs to his wife,
"Has the iceman come yet?" The answer: "No, but he's breathing hard." [Gelb,
831] The end of an era for the iceman as folk hero was marked by a song of minor
popularity in vaudeville whose refrain went: "The Frigidaire can never replace the
Iceman."

good. Only then will they know the peace they instinctively seek. Lazarus's doctrine is a lonely one; he loves humanity, but has little room for tenderness and for individual love. Miriam must follow unnoticed behind him, yearning for the simplicity of her life in the hills of Bethany. Those who accept his paradox, that death is life, lose human contact and the powers of sympathy, hope, humility and belief in man. Caught in the Dionysian ecstasy of his laughter, they throw themselves on the swords of soldiers. It is a chill rendition of Matthew, 10:39: "He who loses his life for my sake will find it."

Hickey's remedy for the ills of the world, as that world is represented by the types in Harry Hope's back room, is equally cold, equally predicated on a belief that human life is an illusion. As Lazarus exhorts, so Hickey, by means of a series of long, brutal individual encounters in the rooms above the bar, forces the dreamers to give over their ultimate link with life, the sustaining pipedream of their worth as human beings. Their dreams hold at least an illusion of life's essence: movement in purposive action. Action, to be sure, will never be taken, but the dreams reveal a basic human truth: to foster life, man must preserve a minimal dream of movement. Hickey, whose promised peace is predicated on showing the dreamers that they will never take action and that their dream of doing so is a lie, brings the peace of death. Like much psychiatric theory, Hickey's Godless theology seeks "adjustment" to a meaningless reality, claiming that he who faces his life will find it. Yet if there is no life to be found, Hickey—not unlike Lazarus—becomes Death's priest.

The world which the dreamers inhabit has the fragile ecology of a tide pool. O'Neill calls the saloon "The Bottom of the Sea Rathskeller," and the imagery of drifting tidal life is pervasive.[5] It is a world that barely holds to the fringes of consciousness, moving hesitantly between sleeping and waking, fusing the two conditions into a continuous trance-like existence. The light that filters through the dirty windows from the street is pale and insufficient to separate day from night. Time is meaningless. Voices are nearly unheard in the comatose silence. Existence at Harry Hope's is reduced to its lowest denominator, a hibernation of animals huddled together in dread of waking.

The dreamers have come to Hope's because, ostensibly, they are failures in the outside world, but their typicality makes it impossible to read their communal condition in terms of indi-

[5]Interestingly, no one of the cast of characters has any connection with the sea, as if O'Neill were deliberately denying the source of his earlier poetic dreams.

vidual weakness. What lies outside is a world without value, a hostile society to which no man can possibly belong, and from which they must take refuge. At one point, Hickey mocks one of the men, saying, "You can't hang around all day looking as if you were scared the street outside would bite you!" But the menace in the streets is real. The threatening automobile that Harry Hope conjures up to justify his failure to take the walk around the neighborhood is, however imaginary, real. It is a symbol of a mechanized, animalistic, spiritless world, a world in which God is dead.

After the long, poetically oriented quest which he had conducted through the plays of the 1920's, seeking a God to which men could belong, O'Neill at last has come to agree with Nietzsche that men live in a Godless world. There is no longer the possibility of being possessed by Dionysian ecstasy. Men's dreams can have no fulfillment that is not in itself illusion; the mindless, unpoetic materialism of each of the dreams is sufficient testimony to the fact that in all the outer world there is nowhere to go, nothing worth having, nothing to which man may make offering as to a God. In the wake of Hickey's teaching, men are left as walking corpses wandering in an icy hell; all they can do is to wait for death. In *Waiting for Godot,* Samuel Beckett describes the same interminable course of life, as Gogo and Didi indulge in senseless repetitious discourse and vaudeville routines to pass time. The pipe-dreams of O'Neill's characters have the same function: they make life tolerable while the dreamers wait for Hickey or Death. As much as each of the dreamers permits himself to understand anything, he knows that the pipe-dreams, his own included, are a game, that they are not real. Each man mocks the dreams of the others as insubstantial and illusory, but the mockery is a defensive irony, an essential element of the self-identification the individual's dreams provide. What cannot be admitted is pity, for pity would acknowledge the truth each seeks to conceal from himself. Nietzsche said God died of such pity; in self-pity the lowest creature will come to despair.

For the dreamers, a deliberately fostered illusion is the sign of membership in the club. The subject of the pipe-dream is unimportant. Some dreams, like Hugo Kalmar's incoherent anarchist ravings, are little more than fragmented, formless memories, holding so little sense of life as to be meaningless. But whether or not the dream is coherent and contains a goal of action, its value lies less in its shape than in the fact that it forms part of the structure of illusion that "gives life to the whole misbegotten mad lot" of dreamers. The saving possibility is the mutuality of the dreamers' condition, for the conjunction of the dreams, the body heat of sleeping animals, provides the warmth of the world. This fact too makes it possible for the dreamers to hope without desire.

The world in which they live exists beyond desire. Whiskey alone sustains physical life. Hunger for food is not expressed, and notably no movement of sexual desire disturbs the quiet. The three whores arouse no one to lust, nor do they try to become objects of desire among the dreamers. Even the proposed marriage of Chuck and Cora is based on other dreams than that of sexual gratification. Very different from the cycle plays, where sexual battles are fought to the death in an arena of passion, Hope's saloon is a world without women. Nevertheless, as in the cycle plays, the power of woman is felt, and here, too, it is a destructive power.

Hickey's wife, Evelyn, is dead. Rosa Parritt, Don Parritt's mother and Larry Slade's former mistress, has gone to the death of spirit her imprisonment will bring upon her. Yet the power of these women, carried into the dreamers' world by the men who have loved them, destroys for a time the structure of life fostered there. In the cycle plays, Deborah and Sara attempt to use Simon, to destroy his dreams and rid themselves of his desire. Rosa Parritt is pictured as an independent, fierce-willed woman who has held possessively onto her son at the same time as she has refused his love. His claim is that she has forced him into the radical movement, yet has permitted him no freedom of mature judgment. At the same time, he makes clear that he wants her to be his mother and resents her flaunting her lovers in the name of "Free Love." Her lover, Larry Slade, has left her in anger, calling her whore, for much the same reason, so that a bond between Larry and Parritt exists that is like, if it is not in fact, that between father and son,[6] and both feel guilty at having betrayed Rosa in order to be free of her rejection of their love. To love Rosa, a man must submit himself completely to her ambitions, but must make no demands in return. Betrayal is a defensive movement of their individuality.

On the other hand, Hickey's wife has made no ostensible demands on her husband. Hickey's description of her conveys the image of a gentle creature, the opposite of Rosa Parritt, but one who in a different way saps a man's individuality. She asks

---

[6]Larry has stood *in loco parentis* to Parritt. Whether or not he is actually Parritt's father is deliberately left ambiguous. Slade denies it when Parritt suggests that he is, but with such vehemence as to raise the possibility.

nothing, fears her husband's attention, yet her capacity for forgiveness, her confident faith in him proves to be as destructive as Rosa's independence. Like Margaret in *The Great God Brown*, Evelyn cannot see what is behind Hickey's face, even when he forces her brutally to look upon it. The blindness of her love makes Hickey live true to her dreams of him and fills him with guilt when he betrays her, just as Parritt and Slade are guilty in their compulsive betrayal of Rosa. O'Neill in the past, sensing that man must belong to some force that controls his being, had shown that those who ran from such possession were in the end caught and destroyed by it. In *The Iceman Cometh,* as in the cycle plays, the force, devoid of its theological implications and reduced to a sexual relationship, has the same effect. Parritt has betrayed his mother to the police, Hickey has murdered Evelyn, and Larry must send his "son" to his death to end his torment, resigning himself finally to the sort of living punishment that Lavinia Mannon accepts. Each seeks death as the only way of assuaging or atoning for the guilt the woman has thrust upon him. Had Simon survived his final rejection by Deborah, something of the same death-leaning emptiness might well have overtaken him.

The three betrayers are the only occupants of the saloon who need pity. They epitomize, perhaps, the men without dreams who live in the hostile streets beyond the barroom door. They come, at least, from such a world, and disturb the dreaming sea. Both Hickey and Parritt force pity into the waters, but it is pity without tenderness. Parritt demands that Slade take pity on him and punish him by commanding him to suicide. Hickey, who insists that Larry's instinctive sympathy for the dreamers is the wrong kind of pity, attempts to rip off their masks and free them of the torture of hope. The play charts his failure and notes as well the way returning illusion brings life again to the sterile waters. When he has gone, old currents move again at the bottom of the sea, and the men who have been wakened to a hideous and intolerable truth begin to dream again.

Hickey's therapy, through different means, is worked on Cornelius Melody. When his role as the romantic soldier is taken from him, he like the bums becomes a comatose, dying animal. He saves himself by assuming another role, as the bums reclothe themselves in illusions. Deborah Harford, too, enters a world like Hope's saloon when she enters the summer house at the end of *More Stately Mansions*, but she must live alone, in the isolation of insanity. Deborah's end is so dark as to be indiscernible.

The Iceman Cometh, however, is illuminated by "darkness visible," and it reflects the despair O'Neill himself felt in the year of its composition. On September 11, 1939, he wrote to Langner from Tao House:

> The whole business from 1918 to now has been so criminally, hoggishly stupid. That is what sticks in one's gorge, that man can never learn but must be always the same old God damned greedy, murderous, suicidal ass! I foresee a world in which any lover of liberty will continue to live with reluctance and be relieved to die.

That it would be a relief to die! The desire that surges to the surface of the lives of the three betrayers in the play was a common reaction in that year. O'Neill was not alone.

The death of the human spirit remained his theme. Shortly, he set to work on a play entitled *The Last Conquest:* "The World-Dictator fantasy of a possible future, and the attempted last campaign of Evil to stamp out even the unconscious memory of Good in Man's spirit. . . ."[7] But the play remained in scenario, and *The Iceman Cometh* was withheld from production because, as he told Langner, "A New York audience could neither see nor hear its meaning. The pity and tragedy of defensive pipe dreams would be deemed downright unpatriotic. . . . But after the war is over, I am afraid . . . that American audiences will understand a lot of *The Iceman Cometh* only too well."

[7]O'Neill to Dudley Nichols, December 16, 1942. He had worked on the outline and scenario over the year prior to the bombing of Pearl Harbor.

Robert J. Andreach

O'Neill's Women in The Iceman Cometh

Eugene O'Neill is generally regarded as America's most important dramatist and *The Iceman Cometh* as one of his three or four finest plays.

In vew of these judgments and the man-God theme that is a standard approach in O'Neill criticism, it is surprising that there is hardly any discussion of the theological frame of reference which the play itself establishes by containing a past that cannot be redeemed, man's nature that cannot be transformed, hope that is really an illusion, and females whose names make them figures of the Blessed Virgin. I am not suggesting that other ways of studying the play are not valid, but I believe any interpretation that ignores the relation between nature and grace and Mary's role in obtaining grace is incomplete. I propose, therefore, to examine the theological implications of *The Iceman Cometh* to explain why O'Neill's males have ambivalent feelings toward Mary and all females, who are figures of Mary.[1]

The inhabitants of Harry Hope's bar are trying to escape their consciousness of their pasts by drinking themselves into unconsciousness or by pretending their pasts were different from what they were or by constructing pipe dreams that their futures will be different from their pasts. Into the bar comes Hickey with one of the oldest precepts of Western culture: "Know yourself."

[1]Robert Brustein, *The Theatre of Revolt* (Boston, 1964), pp. 339–348 and Cyrus Day, "The Iceman and the Bridegroom," *MD,* I (May 1958), 3–9 are two studies which discuss the theological implications. Other excellent studies of the play are Leonard Chabrowe, "Dionysus in *The Iceman Cometh*," *MD,* IV (February 1962), 377–388; Edwin A. Engel, *The Haunted Heroes of Eugene O'Neill* (Cambridge, 1953), pp. 281–296; Doris V. Falk, *Eugene O'Neill and the Tragic Tension* (New Brunswick, 1958), pp. 156–165; Vivian C. Hopkins, " 'The Iceman' Seen Through 'The Lower Depths,' " *CE,* XI (November 1949), 81–87; Helen Muchnic, "Circe's Swine: Plays by Gorky and O'Neill," *CL,* III (Spring, 1951), 119–128; and Rudolf Stamm, "A New Play by Eugene O'Neill," *English Studies,* XXIX (October 1948), 138–145. The work of Carpenter and Straumann will be noted at more appropriate places in the text.

From Renascence, *XVIII (Winter 1966). Reprinted by permission.*

Hickey is wrong, though, for the play reveals that the truth about a man is intolerable and not because of what a human being has been: a pimp, whore, betrayer, drunkard, or murderer, but because of what a human being is: a fallen nature with no hope of redemption.

Self-knowledge is a curse for O'Neill because man is capable of knowing himself but he can do nothing about himself. The future will be the same as the past because man's nature is unaided by grace, and human nature is, in the words of Larry, "a mixture of mud and manure" (1).[2] Yet O'Neill believes man cannot live without hope either; the yearning for something beyond himself is part of his nature too.[3] Since man cannot tolerate the truth because it is hopeless, he constructs illusions, pipe dreams. This brings us to the role of the female in *The Iceman Cometh*.

In the play the simpler, less conscious characters get drunk faster, stay drunk longer, and leave the bar sooner to face reality because they have less consciousness of reality, although, like the others, they refuse to accept the truth about themselves except when Hickey forces them to. The other characters, the last ones to leave the bar or those who do not leave, are distinguished by their consciousness of the role of the female. The last three to leave are Willie, Jimmy, and Harry.

Willie's ditty about the mariner seeking a tavern for gin indicates his recognition, however slight, of the intervention of the female in a man's life. After singing the stanza in which the damsel with "bright blue eyes" appears, he remarks, "And now the influence of a good woman enters our mariner's life." She calls him in to show him "the prettiest *(Rap, rap, rap)*/That ever you did see" (I).

Jimmy's pipe dreams are that his wife Marjorie's infidelity drove him to drink and that "tomorrow" he will pull himself together and return to work. The truth he cannot bear is that he was a drunkard before he was married whose drinking drove her to adultery. He has only a vague recollection of her, finding it "impossible to believe she loved" him (IV).

Harry's pipe dreams are that following his wife Bessie's death he took to drinking in the back room of his bar and that "tomorrow" he will once again walk around the ward seeing his

---

[2]All quotations from *The Iceman Cometh* are taken from the Random House edition (New York, 1946). Italics indicate stage directions.

[3]For a short discussion of the conflict in O'Neill's plays as that between determinism-pragmatism and a search for values based on an ethico-religious tradition, see Heinrich Straumann, *American Literature in the Twentieth Century*, 3rd rev. ed. (New York: Harper Torchbooks, 1965), pp. 183–189.

friends. The truth, as Hickey reminds him, is that "she was always on your neck, making you have ambition and go out and do things, when all you wanted was to get drunk in peace" (III).

From this progression we can begin to see the role of the female. She enters a man's life calling upon him to become more than he is, but by so doing, she makes him feel guilty because he cannot. As a result she becomes an object of hatred to him: a "nagging bitch" to Harry (III), a "damned bitch" to Hickey and Parritt (IV).

The three who do not leave the bar are Parritt, Hickey, and Larry. Parritt's pipe dreams are, first, that he betrayed his mother for patriotic reasons and, second, that he did it for money. Until Act IV he insists he loves her. Then he "confesses" to Larry: "It was because I hated her." Here we have the heart of the problem. The female's love for the male—in this case, the mother for a son—expects him to be more than he is. Since Parritt cannot be more than "a mixture of mud and manure," he comes to hate her for making him feel guilty for not being what she expects, just as his love for his mother makes her feel guilty for not being more than a whore: "After all, I'm her only kid. She used to spoil me and make a pet of me. Once in a great while, I mean. When she remembered me. As if she wanted to make up for something. As if she felt guilty. So she must have loved me a little, even if she never let it interfere with her freedom" (III). But imprisoning her does not remove the guilt. His death does that. When Larry sentences Parritt, he replies, "Thanks, Larry. I just wanted to be sure. I can see now it's the only possible way I can ever get free from her. I guess I've really known that all my life." He knows there is no redemption for him.

Hickey has two pipe dreams, but we will delay examining the second one until later. The first is that he loved his wife, Evelyn. Actually he hated her as well because her love made him feel guilty. That is, she expected him to be more than he is. Her love blinded her to the truth that Hickey cannot be more than he is, and the more she loved him the more guilt and hatred he felt (and still feels) because she could not see what he is: "I even caught myself hating her for making me hate myself so much. There's a limit to the guilt you can feel and the forgiveness and the pity you can take!" (IV).

If imprisoning the one who loved does not remove the guilt, neither does murdering her. Parritt and Hickey are tormented by the memories of the mother and the wife. The mother's eyes seem to follow Parritt everywhere wishing he were dead. When the others shout to Hickey that they are not interested in his confession, he answers, "I don't need to tell anyone. I don't feel guilty. I'm only worried about you." However, a few minutes later he *"suddenly bursts out:* I've got to tell you!" (IV).

Chuck and Cora are good examples of the way love destroys each one's hope. To argue that they can be happy so long as they delude themselves that "tomorrow" they will be married all the while they continue living as they are is to miss the meaning of the play. Chuck hopes he can be more than a drunkard and a pimp, and Cora hopes she can be more than a prostitute. Because each one has this hope as part of his nature, each yearns for something above his present state. Marriage would prove to each that he can be more than he is—that there is a basis for his hope. But since Cora wants to be married, she wants Chuck to be a good husband, just as she wants to be a good wife, and since Chuck wants to be married, he wants Cora to be a good wife, just as he wants to be a good husband. She expects he will stop pimping and drinking; he expects she will stop whoring. The closer they come to marriage the more each one proves once again to the other that there is no hope. Cora's desire to marry, which Chuck hopes for because it will prove he is worthy of being loved and capable of marriage, demonstrates he is nothing more than a drunkard and a pimp, which temporarily destroys his hope that he can be more. Chuck's desire to marry, which Cora hopes for because it will prove she is worthy of being loved and capable of marriage, demonstrates she is nothing more than a prostitute, which temporarily destroys her hope that she can be more. The closer they come to marriage, the more they expect of each other, and since neither is capable of rising to the expectations, the more they hate each other for making each one see the hopeless truth about himself. Yet since they will continue to hope they can be married, they will continue to move toward marriage and, consequently, they will continue to love and hate each other. The alternatives are death or despair.

If Hickey—or any one of the characters—admits he hates the female, he must then admit he has a reason for hating her: she destroyed his hope. This admission is unendurable—except for someone like Parritt, who commits suicide immediately after making it—not merely because each would then have to admit that he is a derelict, which each is willing to do, but because the one who loved him hoped he would be different, which is precisely what each one has always been hoping (part of his nature). To be loved made each one aware of the impossibility of exactly what he has been hoping for himself. Love asks the impossible— that the loved one will rise above his nature—making a pipe dream of the hope each has that he can rise above his nature. Hence each one's guilt because he cannot be other than himself to the one who wants him to be more than himself and hence each one's love for the one who thought enough of him to love him and hatred for her for constantly making him aware that his hope that he can rise above himself is an illusion. The truth is hideous; it forces each character to accept his past and to discard the illusion that "tomorrow" he will be different. It also forces each character to remember that at one time someone loved him enough to ask him to be different.

Larry's pipe dreams are that he no longer cares about life and that he waits for death. Since each pipe dream is invariably the reverse of the truth, his pipe dreams mean that he clings to life and people. He still loves Rosa Parritt, although by walking out on her, he keeps his love a secret, an accusation Parritt hurls at him in Act III. The more the son talks about his mother and his hatred of whores, the closer he takes Larry to the truth until Larry knows that his hope is a pipe dream. He finally confesses to himself that she will never be anything but a whore. Denied his one hope, he falls into despair.

When Parritt comes to Larry with love, calling him father, he makes Larry hate him because Parritt's desire that he understand him forces him to confront the truth. By stripping Larry of his one hope—that he can be more than a drunkard whose love for the mother will redeem himself and her—Parritt brings Larry's vengeance on his head: "Go! Get the hell out of life, God damn you, before I choke it out of you!" (IV). At the same time Parritt makes Larry see that his professed detachment from life is simply another pipe dream.

If this were the extent of the play, it would be a very powerful drama about man's need for illusions in a hopeless universe, but it would not explain why life is hopeless. For this explanation we must turn to the frame of reference the play itself provides. To dramatize the relation between nature and hope is to dramatize the relation between nature and grace and the roles of Christ and Mary in securing grace for man.

Man's hope that he can possess God is based on his faith that God is assisting him through grace to love Him more, for He is the ultimate end of faith, hope, and charity. Christ, the Mediator, is the source of grace dwelling within man, and Mary, the Mother of Christ and therefore the Mother of Redemption, is the Mediatrix of all graces. If grace is not a reality, then man has no hope of salvation because he is thrown back upon his nature, which, despite its faculties and endowments, can never achieve anything other than a natural end, since grace is a gift gratuitously bestowed by God on man, who neither merits nor deserves it, lovingly calling him to a supernatural end, God Himself. Grace is grafted onto the nature of man transforming him interiorly, disposing him to consent freely to Christ's action which is already in him. And man can always pray to Mary to intercede with her Son for further assistance. She is Mary, full of grace, who obtains for us and distributes to us all graces.

Without grace man has no hope of a supernatural end, yet one of the premises of *The Iceman Cometh,* like the rest of O'Neill's plays, is that man's nature is such that he yearns for something beyond the horizon. A few minutes after his arrival Hickey announces that by accepting the truth about himself he has rid himself of every "single damned hope or dream" that nagged him. Claiming he has achieved "peace," he criticizes Larry for showing the wrong kind of pity, the kind that encourages the false hope of illusions. This is his second pipe dream: once men accept the truth about themselves they will throw away their false or lying hopes and find real hope. The fact that Hickey, like all men, needs hope in order to live is dramatized in his relationship with Harry Hope.

At the start of the birthday party Hickey *"grabs* Hope's *hand and pumps it up and down."* He *"slaps* Hope *on the back encouragingly."* He *"looks up the table at* Hope," toasting him with these words: "And I mean it when I say I hope today will be the biggest day in your life, and in the lives of everyone here, the beginning of a new life of peace and contentment where no pipe dreams can ever nag at you again" (II).

Act III is the climax. Hickey and Hope enter together with the former clapping the latter *"encouragingly on the shoulder,"* preparing him for his walk outside. When Harry returns Hickey puts his *"hand on his shoulder—kindly."* He then *"pats his shoulder—coaxingly."* But the pipe dream is exploding, for the instant Harry sheds his false hope and faces reality, he feels "like a corpse." Harry does not discover real hope; he does not become a "new man" as Hickey hoped he would; he becomes a dead man. The meaning of this act is that Hickey's quest for truth is a movement toward death. Because he wants to believe there is real hope for man, Hickey *"calls to* Hope *coaxingly:* How's it coming, Governor? Beginning to feel free, aren't you? Relieved and not guilty any more?" But since real hope is the greatest of all pipe dreams, both Hope and whiskey are dead at this point. Act III ends with Hickey *"gazing with worried kindliness at* Hope," trying to convince himself and Harry that there is real hope in life.

Act IV makes it absolutely clear that Hope does not come alive until he creates the false but necessary hope of an illusion.

In Act IV as soon as Hickey denies he hates Evelyn, which he has just blurted out as the reason he murdered her, *"his eyes fix on* Hope." He insists he must have been insane. Hope's *"face lights up, as if he were grasping at some dawning hope in his mind,"* because he and the others can use Hickey's "insanity." Hickey *"pleads"* with Hope: "You know I couldn't say that to Evelyn, don't you, Harry—unless—." Hope *"eagerly"* seizes this, *"jubilant"* that Hickey has provided them with a pipe dream. After Hickey leaves Hope says *"hopefully"* about the whiskey: "Bejees, maybe it'll have the old kick, now he's gone." Hickey finally knows that the only hope given to man is the false hope that "tomorrow" will be different and if one does not construct this kind of hope to assuage his yearnings, he must either die or fall into despair. Therefore he leaves to go to his death.

Now that we know why O'Neill's universe is hopeless and why men need illusions, we can examine the role of the female and the love-hate theme. By giving the females the names they have, O'Neill makes them figures of the Blessed Virgin Mary. Cora is short for Corinna, which means maiden. Margie is a diminutive of Marjorie, a variation of Margaret, which means pearl.

The symbolic use of gems is a very old tradition which culminates in medieval literature. The pearl is a symbol of purity, preciousness, and virginity. In the late fourteenth-century poem, *Pearl,* the poet, grieving for his lost pearl, awakens in a dream to see her across a river. When he expresses his wish to join her, she rebukes him because as she expounds the doctrine of salvation by grace, including the roles of Christ and Mary, she makes him realize she is a queen of Heaven, a figure of Mary, and he, a sinner of the earth separated from God and his pearl by an untainted stream. Ever since Adam's fall the river must be crossed by the way of death. She reminds him of man's hope by allowing him a vision of the New Jerusalem, where the bleeding Christ leads the procession to the throne of God the Father. In Thomas Usk's *Testament of Love* the pearl, figured as a woman named Margaret, denotes grace, learning or wisdom of God, and the Church.[4]

[4]For convenient summaries of the Margaret–pearl symbolism, see S. K. Heninger, Jr., "The Margarite-Pearl Allegory in Thomas Usk's *Testament of Love," Speculum,* XXXIII (January 1957), 92–98 and *Pearl,* ed. E. V. Gordon (Oxford, 1953), xxvii–xxxvi.

Additional evidence that O'Neill is using the pearl symbolism is given in Larry's mocking summary of what Hickey
correctly claims is Larry's prayer: "Beloved Christ, let me live a
little longer at any price! If it's only for a few days more, or a few
hours even, have mercy, Almighty God, and let me still clutch
greedily to my yellow heart this sweet treasure, this jewel beyond
price, the dirty, stinking bit of withered old flesh which is my
beautiful little life!" (III). The "treasure" and the "jewel beyond
price" allude to the Biblical source for the pearl symbolism,
where the "pearl of great price" represents the pious desire for
Heaven:

> "The kingdom of heaven is like a treasure hidden in a field; he who
> finds it hides it, and in his joy goes and sells all that he has and buys
> that field.
> "Again, the kingdom of heaven is like a merchant in search of fine
> pearls. When he finds a single pearl of great price, he goes and sells
> all that he has and buys it" (Matt. xiii. 44–46).

Of the remaining females, Bessie is a diminutive of
Elizabeth, a kinswoman of Mary, and Rosa is a variation of Rose,
one of the great symbols in Catholic art for Mary. Finally, the
name of the female who befriended Hickey, Mollie, is a diminutive of Mary.

In medieval literature the symbolism of the rose reaches a
high point in Dante. Converting his earthly experience with Beatrice, a real female and a figure of Mary, into a spiritual one,
Dante awakens to the "new life" of the soul. In Canto XXX of
the *Purgatorio* Beatrice appears "within a cloud of flowers" to
guide him to the exfoliating Rose, which includes along the way
an examination on faith, hope, and charity. By the last three
cantos of the *Paradiso,* after leading him to St. Bernard and then
Mary, the Mother of Faith, she takes her rightful place leaving
him free to receive the mystical experience looking into the supreme light of God. [5]

The Iceman Cometh inverts the Beatrice-Pearl figure. Cora,
Margie, and Pearl are three prostitutes frequently twitted about
their loss of virginity. Marjorie is driven to infidelity. Bessie is a
bitch; Mollie, a brothel madame. Rosa has faith, a point made a

[5] O'Neill's familiarity with Dante is most obvious in Scene X of *The Fountain,*
the one in which Beatriz awakens Juan to the illumination that "God is a flower.
..." Although there is much in this play that is not only not from Dante but
antithetical to him, there are enough details to demonstrate O'Neill's familiarity
with the *Commedia.*

few times by her son, but her faith neither prevents him from betraying her nor helps her be more than a whore.

If man tries to escape Mary, our spiritual Mother, by turning to Eve, our physical Mother, he is still no better off in this play. According to St. Augustine and other Church Fathers, Eve is a type of Mary, who is traditionally called the new Eve: as Eve concurred in our fall, Mary collaborates in our redemption. What Evelyn has done to Hickey is what every female who loves has done to a man. She had faith and hope in him, which when added to his yearning, buoyed up his faith and hope in his future: "But there was no shaking Evelyn's belief in me, or her dreams about the future. After each letter of hers, I'd be as full of faith as she was" (IV). Ironically, each act of forgiveness based on her faith and hope that he would become more than the husband he was only made him feel his guilt more for not being a better husband to the woman he loved and only demonstrated to him he could not become a better husband. By proving to him he could not, her love destroyed his hope that he could become a "new man" and created his hatred for her and her pipe dream, causing him to murder her. As a type of Mary, Eve may lead man to Mary, but this is no spiritual ascent because Mary is incapable of aiding him. In fact, her love is destructive.

The men who suffer most in the play are those who have been most affected by the female: Parritt, Hickey. and Larry. Because they have more love, they have more hope than the other men. Parritt hopes to find understanding; Hickey hopes to find real, not false, hope; Larry hopes his love will redeem himself and Rosa. Consequently, each one becomes an object of hatred. Parritt comes to Larry seeking understanding but instead receives his death sentence. Hickey tries to help the others but instead incurs their hatred. By showing pity, Larry prompts Hickey's criticism that his is "bum pity" (III), since it encourages the false hope that pipe dreams bring. Determined not to become involved with Parritt because he suspects the truth, Larry elicits his contempt. In other words, what happens to them is what happens to the female whose love for the male demonstrates that his hope is merely another pipe dream.

Significantly, these three men (and three others[6]) are described as having blue eyes. Blue, the color of romance and

[6]The three are Willie, Lewis, and Wetjoen. The extent of Willie's consciousness will be noted later in this paper. I do not know why the other two have blue eyes. They are considerably less conscious than the three who leave the bar last and the three who do not leave at all. There is only one possibility that I can see,

dreams, identifies them as dreamers, typical O'Neill characters.[7] But since blue is also the Blessed Virgin's color, the play suggests that any man who loves has affinities with the female who loves, a figure of the Blessed Virgin. Larry is the most interesting. He has the most love and pity. He has been able to love Rosa for years, and he has been able to hope for himself and her for years until the confessions of Parritt and Hickey overwhelm him with the truth. It is not coincidental that he has the most blue of the characters; twice he refers to his problem as an excess of blue: "I've got the blues" (I).

Since the women in the play are figures of Mary, the drama in the bar is O'Neill's conception of the universal drama, the essence of which is presented in Act I. When the curtain is raised, all the characters except Larry and Rocky are asleep. Shortly thereafter Willie (who has blue eyes) yells out in his nightmare, "It's a God-damned lie! *(He begins to sob)* Oh, Papa! Jesus!" The others stir, *"but none of them wakes up except* Hope." He is not annoyed, preferring, however, to return to his dream. He tells Rocky to give Willie a drink so that he will sleep. Later Willie comes to, this time to sing his ditty, which awakens the others. Hope is irritated and when Willie sings the line about the damsel with "bright blue eyes" threatens to lock him in his room upstairs. Since Willie promises to be quiet, Hope relents. Awake, Hope and the others indulge in their favorite pipe dreams about "tomorrow" until Willie repeats his ditty. He stops when *"he catches* Hope's *eyes fixed on him condemningly."* Gradually the men fall asleep again just before Pearl, Margie, Chuck, and Cora arrive. Hope has difficulty sleeping, telling Cora to "cut the loud noise!" As soon as Rocky announces that Cora has seen Hickey, Hope is *"instantly wide awake."*

The cry, "Oh, Papa! Jesus!" represents man's hope in the nightmare of life, but it is sobbed only in moments of agony because, since each man knows what he is—Hickey was well aware of what he was before met Evelyn—this is an almost impossible hope. The female as a real woman destroys this hope because her love demonstrates the recipient cannot rise to the

---

although it is far-fetched. They refer to a battle in the Boer War, in which both took part, at the Modder River, and once Hickey calls to them to show some "Modder River spirit" (III). Perhaps O'Neill is punning on *modder-mud* (human nature) and *moeder-mother* (Mary or any female), or perhaps he wants a word that sounds like mother.

[7]For a very thorough discussion of the dreamer in O'Neill's plays, see Frederic I. Carpenter, *American Literature and the Dream* (New York, 1955). See also his book-length study, *Eugene O'Neill,* Twayne's United States Authors Series (New York, 1964).

expectations love creates for him, which is what he has always hoped he could do. The female as a figure of Mary destroys this hope because her love demonstrates the recipient will not receive the grace necessary to him to a supernatural end, which is what he has always hoped he would receive. There is no Son of God, no source of grace, because God withholds the grace necessary for salvation. For O'Neill God is either dead to man's predicament or a sadistic tyrant Who creates man with his nature, offers Mary to him, and then laughs at his yearning to reach Him. The female is as pathetic as the male. She does not know there is no grace, nor does she understand why the men hate her. She continues to pity them, forgive them, and love them in the hope they will become more than "mud and manure." But her hope, like their hope, is the greatest of illusions. It is only by fleeing from Mary and all females or the memory of them or anyone who reminds him of them or anyone who loves and shows pity that man can find any kind of hope. As Hickey learns, man's sole refuge is the false but necessary hope of pipe dreams sustained by whiskey.

Not only does the play invert the Beatrice-Pearl figure, it also inverts the Biblical passage that forms the basis for the title of the play.[8] In Matt. xxv. 1–13 the bridegroom is Christ, Who brings the death that precedes life, the death that makes possible resurrection and union with Him in the marriage feast. In *The Iceman Cometh* the Iceman is death: "Well, by God," says Larry, "it fits, for Death was the Iceman Hickey called to his home!" (III). And the female betrays the marriage by ushering in death. In one of the most ominous passages in the play, Rocky repeats to the others his threat to Hickey: "Remember dat, or you'll wake up in a hospital—or maybe worse, wid your wife and de iceman walkin' slow behind yuh' " (II).

O'Neill's position is summed up by Hickey. Since he has "had hell inside" himself, he maintains he can recognize it in others. He sees "hell" in Parritt, and he knows "it's a woman" who caused it. "The old real love stuff," Hickey asserts, "crucifies" (II). Love crucifies but there is no resurrection. Whereas Beatrice and Pearl lead man to Mary and then Christ, O'Neill's females bring with them, not Christ, but death—final death with no resurrection—or despair—the death of hope. For O'Neill life is hopeless because the past can never be redeemed without the grace necessary to transform man's nature, drawing him beyond the horizon.

[8]Day's article, "The Iceman and the Bridegroom," is especially helpful here.

Timo Tiusanen

Through the Fog into the Monologue
Long Day's Journey into Night

In *Long Day's Journey into Night* O'Neill's reliance on the expressive power of his dialogue is still greater than in *The Iceman Cometh*. He has only five characters in his cast; there is no chorus, nor are there any changes in the setting; there is a most effective return to the repetitive sound effect. In spite of these dissimilarities the dynamics of these two plays work in a similar manner. Instead of transferring from one group of characters to another, O'Neill now goes from one theme to another. There is more variety of theme, less of character; all the four Tyrones stand out as fully individualized human beings, bound together by a common fate, by an inescapable love-hate relationship. This tragedy has four protagonists. When working his way toward the final revelations, toward four magnificent modified monologues, O'Neill employed in his dialogue several solutions we know from *The Iceman Cometh*.

There are, first of all, the masks. Mary Tyrone has two masks in Act I, those of relaxed self-confidence and of nervousness. She is back at home after a cure in a sanatorium for drug addicts; the three Tyrone men have confidence in her ability to resist the temptation this time. Her gradual return to the old habit is the decisive change in the family situation during this long day's journey. It releases unexpected reactions in the others, in the famous actor James Tyrone, in his thirty-three-year-old actor son Jamie, a failure and an alcoholic, and in Edmund, a journalist ten years younger than his brother who is about to be sent to a tuberculosis sanatorium.[1]

[1]It is understandable that those who approach O'Neill from a biographical point of view have found it a matter of interest to compare *Long Day's Journey* with the facts of his life. There are detailed discussions by the Gelbs *(O'Neill,* pp.

"Through the Fog into the Monologue: Long Day's Journey into Night," *In Timo Tiusanen,* O'Neill's Scenic Images *(copyright © 1968 by Princeton University Press), pp. 285–303. Reprinted by persmission of Princeton University Press.*

In Act I there is still hope: the inner struggle is still going on in Mary. Hence the masks, given in the initial description of Mary and in the stage directions between and within the speeches: "What strikes one immediately is her extreme nervousness. Her hands are never still" (LDJ 12). Another fixing point for this mask is her hair: *"(She stops abruptly, catching Jamie's eyes regarding her with an uneasy, probing look. Her smile vanishes and her manner becomes self-conscious)* Why are you staring, Jamie? *(Her hands flutter up to her hair)"* (LDJ 20). The mask is made visible through these means, and there is interaction with changes in the tone of voice, with facial expressions, with the gestures and groupings.

The opening act closes with a pantomime by Mary. She makes the apprehensive men leave her alone, and the tension between her two roles is shown: "Her first reaction is one of relief. She appears to relax. . . . But suddenly she grows terribly tense again. Her eyes open and she strains forward, seized by a fit of nervous panic. She begins a desperate battle with herself. Her long fingers, warped and knotted by rheumatism, drum on the arms of the chair, driven by an insistent life of their own, without her consent" (LDJ 49).

The battle is lost. In the following acts Mary progresses deeper and deeper into the secluded world of a drug addict, swinging all the time between two roles, wearing alternately two masks. When she has her defenses up, no petitions from the others, no events on the stage, can reach her. She is as strangely detached as Deborah. And when she has not yet totally escaped, she feels guilty—of her irrational flight, of the death of one of her sons, called Eugene in the play, of Edmund having been born at all, of life in general. She may confess her concern for Edmund or her fear of consumption, she may speak of her own guilt—only to turn abruptly away again: "Then, catching herself, with an instant change to stubborn denial" (LDJ 88). It is foolish to worry; it is reassuring to cling to the pipe dream that Edmund has only a bad summer cold.

The further Mary recedes from the living room of the Tyrones, the clearer it becomes that her two roles are played

3–8, *et passim)*, by Carpenter (*Eugene O'Neill*, pp. 20–24), and by Raleigh (*The Plays of Eugene O'Neill*, pp. 87–95). What should not be forgotten, however, is that the "truthfulness" or "distortion" of the facts does not matter finally: "the O'Neills have all gone to their graves, while the play remains" (Raleigh, p. 91). Or, to agree with Gierow, the first theater person to read the script: *Long Day's Journey* is a self-dependent work of art, its autobiographical nature does not mean very much (*Introduktioner*, p. 38).

behind the masks of her two different ages. "Her most appealing
quality is the simple, unaffected charm of a shy convent-girl
youthfulness she has never lost—an innate unworldly innocence"
(LDJ 13). When she has escaped, when she wears the mask of
detachment, she lives in her convent days again, far from James
Tyrone and the shabby hotel rooms that have been her surroundings throughout her married life. This movement in the dimension
of time resembles the dynamics in *More Stately Mansions* and
The Iceman Cometh: Mary is a "one-time" convent girl.[2] The
masks, written into the stage directions, are given three different
functions in the case of Mary Tyrone; they show the conflict
between temptation and resistance, between her drugged and
normal states, and between her adolescence and old age.

Mary is the best example of the application made of the
masks in *Long Day's Journey into Night,* yet she is not the only
one. The continuous vacillation between attachment and repul-
sion has been observed by several critics.[3] In fact, each of the
characters wears two masks in his relations to the other members
of the family: those of love and hatred. The play is a chain of
small circles, all touching the areas of mutual sympathy and antagonism, all obeying the mechanics of defenses, accusations,
and counter-accusations. On the stage, the circles are drawn by
the actors: their positions, gestures, vocal and facial expressions.

Temporary harmonies are possible, even between Tyrone
and Jamie, two archenemies: "His son looks at him, for the first
time with an understanding sympathy. It is as if suddenly a deep
bond of common feeling existed between them in which their
antagonisms could be forgotten" (LDJ 36). Yet in the next moment the pendulum swings toward bitter enmity; another circle is
started. A primary vehicle for this incessant movement, in addition to the sudden, paradoxical change of masks, is the clipped
quality of the dialogue. When Hickey was coming close to

[2]Carpenter compares *Long Day's Journey* with *The Emperor Jones:* "The
dramatic progression of the action in present time counterpoints the dramatic
regression of the memory into time past, which in turn develops a progressive
understanding of the psychological motivation within the mind" (p. 93).

[3]"The family, in brief, is chained together by resentment, guilt, recrimination;
yet, the chains that hold it are those of love as well as hate" (Brustein, *The
Theatre of Revolt,* p. 351). Gascoigne speaks of the changes of masks "properly
buried here in the language," and of the entanglement of the characters "by a
network of recriminations" *(Twentieth-Century Drama,* p. 118). Cf. Whitman,
"O'Neill's Search," p. 167; Gassner, *Theatre at the Crossroads,* p. 72; Stamm,
" 'Faithful Realsim,' " p. 244; Waith, "An Exercise in Unmasking," p. 189; Åke
Janzon, *Bonniers Litterära Magasin,* 25, 3 (March 1956), 238; and Dorn, *Er-
lösungsthematik,* pp. 17–27.

dangerous areas, to the mine fields of *The Iceman Cometh,* he interrupted his sentences, giving his listeners only a hint, letting only an uneasy suspicion form in their minds.[4] It is so also in *Long Day's Journey into Night.*

We might speak of five different uses made of the interrupted sentences. Three of them are closely associated with the total dynamics of the play. (1) It is certainly not O'Neill's invention that the adversaries interrupt one another in emotionally tense scenes out of mere excitement; there are such cases in *Long Day's Journey.* (2) Especially in Act I the Tyrones guard one another, preventing the speakers from approaching dangerous subjects of discussion—Edmund's illness, or Mary's newly aroused inclination, revealed by her movements the previous night. It is a family taboo even to suspect that Mary is not completely healed—and another that Edmund might be in real danger. Mary has barely hinted at her feeling that the men are keeping an eye on her when Edmund interrupts, "too vehemently": "I didn't think anything!" (LDJ 47). Or, Jamie has hardy interpreted a remark by Tyrone as an indication that the father is thinking of Edmund's death when he is checked by Tyrone, in a "guiltily explosive" speech (LDJ 34).

(3) They are checked not only by one another but also by themselves. Examples of sentences interrupted by the speaker himself are numerous: the Tyrones often stop themselves right on the threshold of a terrible accusation or self-accusation. They need another drink or shot in the arm to come out with the truth—as they finally do. Before they reach the stage of modified monologues, they exercise introspection by leaving something unsaid. "Please stop staring!" Mary exclaims. "One would think you were accusing me—" (LDJ 68)—of having taken morphine again, she is about to say, but does not dare. Both this and the second usage have two functions: they add to the tension of the play by creating secrets, and they leave an impression that all of the characters know what is about to be revealed. This is not the first time these circles are run through. They are parts of an incessant discussion, parts of a relentless family fate, realized from year to year, from day to day—and into night.

(4) A modification of this, not as dynamic, is the interruption as a result of an overpowering feeling. There is nothing more to

---

[4]"It is precisely the fact that these intimations are not fully understood at the moment of their use which is important from the point of view of the dramatist: the audience has as yet no clear conception of the meaning, a residue of doubt remains, at once disturbing and a source of enhanced concentration" (Clemen on *The Merchant of Venice: The Development of Shakespeare's Imagery,* p. 83).

be added by the speaker; the sentence is complete in its context, even if deficient in its form. Tyrone speaks "shakenly" to Mary after one of her outpourings of accusations against doctors, in spite of Edmund's presence and the delicacy of the theme of death: "Yes, Mary, it's no time—" (LDJ 74).

(5) The last usage, again closely bound to the total dynamics, occurs when one of the four interrupts a speaker, not so much because these two were getting into an argument, as to give a helping hand to a third. "James, do be quiet" (LDJ 22), Mary says to her husband who is reproaching Jamie. As in *More Stately Mansions* there is no end of new frontiers being formed. The boys react against Tyrone (LDJ 77), the parents against their sons, all the men against Mary; the mother defends her sons, each of them at different times. *The Iceman Cometh,* with its massive dynamics, operated with a few emphatic frontiers: the chorus for or against Hickey. *Long Day's Journey into Night,* with its fewer characters, is a more fluid and labile play.

If we start looking for the roots of this kind of dialogue, it is possible to go back as far as to the first fluctuating monologues in O'Neill. The small circles drawn by Yank in *The Hairy Ape* in his efforts to overcome the difficulties of communication have an affinity with the way the Tyrones proceed. The circles are now drawn by several characters in their attempts to understand. The last act of *Welded,* with its precarious harmony and violent accusations, *Strange Interlude,* with its vacillation, and all of the mask plays were important later developments. Essentially, this kind of dialogue has dramatic rather than literary merits: it speaks not with striking verbal images, but with its incessant movement. It has hardly been fully analyzed or appreciated by the literary critics of drama.[5]

It is an abstraction to say that the small circles in *Long Day's Journey into Night* are formed by alternating love and hatred. The concrete elements in a play are its themes: the circles are built out of bits of discussion, mostly reminiscences. Instead of groups of characters, this play has groups of speeches, each around a theme. The topics discussed include Mary's hatred of

[5]Raleigh admits that Edmund is "capable, sporadically, of a certain eloquence" (p. 235) and says that O'Neill learned "three things: the necessity for restraint, the tonic value of irony, and, the *sine qua non* for the drama, propriety of speech to speaker" (p. 237–38). Yet the scenic merits of the dialogue are not duly considered; to Raleigh, "the plays are but words on pages, as is all literature finally, and the words themselves very often have little about them that can be called distinctive" (p. 236).

doctors, her convent days, her intolerable life in shabby hotels; Tyrone's stinginess, his hard childhood, his drinking habits; Jamie's failure, in all its varied aspects; Edmund's illness, his rebellious opinions on politics and literature, his experiences on the sea. None of these themes is given a conclusive treatment in the first three acts of the play: again, O'Neill is a careful builder of drama.

One theme is taken up and developed to an emotional climax, then there is a standstill until a new theme is picked up, to be treated in a similar way.[6] This is a picture of O'Neill's total development, too: he picked up a certain scenic means of expression, developed it (often to an overuse), and then began working with another. Near the end of his career, he drew his means of expression together—as he did the themes of *Long Day's Journey*.

Even if the emphasis is on the dialogue, it is necessary to pay attention to the interaction of several scenic means of expression. The autobiographical character of the setting is of lesser interest to us than its functional aspects. One of the bookshelves may include most of the books young O'Neill read and admired; this is not, however, of great significance because their names and authors can hardly be made visible to the audience. The relation between Mary and the setting is, on the other hand, interesting: the house is inescapable to her, more so than to the others.[7] We never see Mary leave the house; we know that when she goes out it is only to fetch more morphine. As a contrast, the departures of the men are demonstrated on the stage. Tyrone and Jamie go out to cut the hedge; Edmund takes a walk in the fog, escaping into his poetic vision; all three go downtown, have company, and come home drunk. They do come home—to carry the burden of their family fate.

Mary is deserted by the men: this is the impression conveyed by leaving her alone on the stage at the end of two scenes. Act I is closed with Mary's pantomime, quoted above. She is left even more emphatically alone at the close of II, ii, when Edmund leaves her in the living room, Tyrone and Jamie shout their

---

[6]Clemen remarks that independent parts can be separated from the novels or epic poems, while the "texture of the drama is of a much closer web, and the necessity of an inner continuity, of a mutual cooperation and connection of all parts is greater in drama. . . . In a truly great drama nothing is left disconnected, everything is carred on" (p. 6).

[7]Cf. Brustein on the existential drama: "But even when the setting is relatively realistic—as in the plays of Pirandello, Brecht, and O'Neill—the claustrophobic atmosphere is just as oppressive" (p. 32).

"Goodbye, Mary" and "Goodbye, Mama" from the hall. She sighs with relief—only to go to the other extreme and give her curtain line: "Then Mother of God, why do I feel so lonely?" (LDJ 95). Whether to call this desertion symbolic or not is a pure conjecture; one might say that it is both completely realistic and deeply symbolic, at the same time. In fact, this is the way all scenic means of expression are employed in *Long Day's Journey into Night:* they have a multiple motivation, both realistic and symbolic.[8]

All the outer world means to Mary is a place from which she can obtain drugs. James is the only one of the four who has contacts with the "respectable" people in the town: he can go on talking with them, even forgetting his family and the waiting meal in doing so. The specific place of action, between back and front parlors, is interpreted by Doris V. Falk: "The family 'lives' in that mid-region between the bright formality of the exterior front parlor—the mask—and the little-known dark of the rear-room."[9] In addition to these symbolic overtones belonging to the setting as a whole, there is a significance attached to the rooms upstairs, where Mary is known or suspected to be drugging herself. Her character is firmly established in the first three acts, where she leaves the stage only to go into the two parlors and through the front parlor upstairs—so firmly established, in fact, that it is more suggestive to keep her off-stage through most of Act IV. All that reminds us of her are references in the dialogue and the noise of her steps. Mary lives in the imagination of the audience—to come and make her shocking entrance at the end of the play.

There is an interaction between the setting, the foghorn, and Mary's modified monologue in Act III, in a scenic image that might be called a preliminary synthesis of Mary's role. She is again alone, right in the focus of interest; she has reached the stage of frankly confessional monologues earlier than the men; and then the foghorn comes, with its gloomy message of hopelessness. She has used Cathleen, the "second girl," as an excuse for her modified monologue, indicating how little choice she has in her search for human contacts.[10] Now she is without company and relaxes, her fingers calm. Even the pause is recorded, as elsewhere in the play: "It is growing dark in the room.

---

[8]Clemen has spoken of the "deeply organic nature" of Shakespeare's verbal images in the balcony scene of *Romeo and Juliet:* "So everything in this image has a double function: the clouds and the heavenly messengers may be reality, and at the same time they are symbols" (p. 67).

[9]Doris V. Falk, *Eugene O'Neill and the Tragic Tension*, p. 181.

[10]Cf. Raleigh, p. 104.

There is a pause of dead quiet. Then from the world outside comes the melancholy moan of the foghorn, followed by a chorus of bells, muffled by the fog, from the anchored craft in the harbor. Mary's face gives no sign she has heard, but her hands jerk and the fingers automatically play for a moment on the air. . . . She suddenly loses all the girlish quality and is an aging, cynically sad, embittered woman" (LDJ 107). Mary's shift from one rôle to another is given an emphatic treatment here by using the movements of her fingers and reminding us, once again, of one of her dreams: to become a concert pianist. In her monologue she expresses her disillusionment: not even the Blessed Virgin, whose consolation is her dearest pipe dream, cares to help a dope fiend. She has just decided to go and get some more morphine when the men come in, to end the scenic image, to relieve her from the joy and burden of loneliness, and to start the circular movement again.

The presence of the fog is conveyed to the audience through the foghorn and through references in the dialogue. Mary's attitude is typically ambivalent: the fog is both a disguise from the world and a symbol of her guilty escape.[11] "It hides you from the world and the world from you," she explains to Cathleen. "You feel that everything has changed, and nothing is what it seemed to be. No one can find or touch you any more. . . . It's the foghorn I hate. It won't let you alone. It keeps reminding you, and warning you, and calling you back" (LDJ 98–99). Edmund has experienced the same fascination of escape during his walk in the fog: "Everything looked and sounded unreal. Nothing was what it is. That's what I wanted—to be alone with myself in another world where truth is untrue and life can hide from itself. . . . Who wants to see life as it is, if they can help it?" (LDJ 131). Yet Edmund comes back from the fog to describe his experience, to give it a verbal form, to turn it into art.[12]

O'Neill specifies the use of the foghorn, with its connotations of fascination and dread, of fate and unreality, at three phases during the play. One of them is discussed above; one is an

[11]As Raleigh remarks, the fog both forms "a profound, brooding, and steadily deepening, natural backdrop for the various tragedies of the Tyrones," and represents "that blessed loss of identity for which all the main characters, the father excepted, are seeking" (p. 24).

[12]"For the playwright has discovered another escape besides alcohol, Nirvana, or death from the terrible chaos of life: the escape of art where chaos is ordered and the meaningless made meaningful. The play itself is an act of forgiveness and reconciliation, the artist's lifelong resentment disintegrated through complete understanding of the past and total self-honesty" (Brustein, pp. 355–56).

introductory usage at the beginning of Act III; the third will be discussed in this paragraph. Elsewhere, the foghorn is utilized as a kind of repetitive sound coulisse, to be resorted to according to the judgment of the stage director. In a scene between Mary and Edmund we have a beautiful example of O'Neill's sense of drama, in his transference from human expression into the foghorn. Edmund has voiced his bitterest accusation ("It's pretty hard to take at times, having a dope fiend for a mother!"), and immediately asks for forgiveness after seeing his mother's reaction—all life seems "to drain from her face, leaving it with the appearance of a plaster cast." There is a standstill, the emotion cannot be developed further; and this is where the foghorn is employed: *"(There is a pause in which the foghorn and the ships' bells are heard.)* Mary *(Goes slowly to the windows at right like an automaton—looking out, a blank far-off quality in her voice).* Just listen to that awful foghorn. And the bells. Why is it fog makes everything sound so sad and lost, I wonder?" (LDJ 120–21). Another familiar scenic unit employed is the automaton effect, also met occasionally in *Long Day's Journey into Night.* As to this scenic image as a whole, we might speak of the old principle of *"pars pro toto"*: O'Neill needed a sense of the total tragedy between mother and son, and evoked it by giving a concrete part of it—the noise of the foghorn.

The theme of the fog is given even a comic treatment in Jamie's homecoming. "The fron [sic] steps tried to trample on me," he complains in the beginning of his drunken and grotesquely comic appearance. "Took advantage of fog to waylay me. Ought to be a lighthouse out there" (LDJ 155). It is worth emphasizing that *Long Day's Journey into Night* is not void of comedy.[13] One of the functions of Cathleen is to provide comic relief. She also plays confidante to Mary and has a choral function: "He's a fine gentleman," she says of Tyrone, "and you're a lucky woman" (LDJ 106). This is how the Tyrones must look in the eyes of outsiders; yet the opinion has an ironical effect in its context. So has her innocent remark somewhat earlier in the scene: "You've taken some of the medicine? It made you act funny, Ma'am" (LDJ 104). One of the excuses, here, as well as in *The Iceman Cometh,* is an unconvincing effort to be jocular—

---

[13] "'Comic relief' has a crude sound; but, to some degree and in some form or other, the thing it suggests is a necessity" (Granville-Barker, *Prefaces,* I, 310). On the "comic relief" in *Long Day's Journey* cf. Brustein, p. 351, Carpenter, p. 152.

afterwards. Insults are "only teasing" or "only kidding" (LDJ 42, 90).

Tyrone and Edmund begin to play cards early in Act IV. But the compulsions to confess, to find sympathy, are stronger than the merely mechanical act of handling the cards. Tyrone begins to speak about the play he bought, and how he guaranteed his economic success and artistic failure with it: no one wanted to see him in any other role. Then he "glances vaguely at his cards" and asks: "My play, isn't it?" (LDJ 150). The intention is bitterly ironic: this is what is left of Tyrone's play, of his life—a handful of cards.

Stage action and groupings also interact with dialogue elsewhere. When Mary has taken her first dose of drug, everyone avoids looking at her. She herself goes behind Edmund, the most innocent and least suspicious of her men, to save him from the observation as long as possible (LDJ 58). Two situations are repeated with variation, to show how Mary's position is changed by her fall. Tyrone, the closest person to her, enters together with her in Act I—and follows behind her in II, ii, in a similar entrance after a meal. He keeps beside Mary in their exit at the end of II, i—and remains on the stage in Act III after her exit "as if not knowing what to do. He is a sad, bewildered, broken old man. He walks wearily off" (LDJ 123). These changes occur in emphatic phases of the play; they are important indications of development in the relations between the characters. So is the scattered grouping at the beginning of II, ii. Tyrone and Jamie look out of the door and the window; Edmund sits so that he does not have to watch his mother (LDJ 71). The family is falling apart.

A special feature in *Long Day's Journey into Night* is its plentiful quotations,[14] most of which appear in Act IV. They prepare the way for the confessions, they accentuate the tragic feeling created by the modified monologues. Leech is worried about O'Neill's taste when choosing the poems: "it appears they are quoted *con amore,* with the implication that they represent what poetry exclusively is."[15] On the other hand, they are quoted

[14]Raleigh says that O'Neill uses quotations "both to create a cultural continuum" and to characterize the Tyrones (p. 230). To James Tyrone, Shakespeare is an "optimistic moralizer," while his sons are steeped in "degenerate" European writers, distasteful to their father. Jamie uses Shakespeare "as one of his many weapons in his endless verbal war with his father"; and "there is a design to his literary quotations: hate is Shakespeare; boisterousness is Kipling; elegy is Wilde, Rossetti, and above all, Swinburne" (p. 232).

[15]Leech, *Eugene O'Neill,* p. 57.

both seriously and parodically. O'Neill is on his guard against sentimentality in this late play: before he reaches pathos, he turns around by using a sudden ironic twist. And there is no doubt that the quotations fulfill their basic function, described by Sigvard Mårtensson: they make it possible for the playwright to "express the elevated emotion, the strong tension otherwise not easily articulated by the realistic dialogue. The technique is employed with distinction and never breaks the frame."[16] It is quite natural to quote poetry in a family of two actors and a would-be author.

The central problem of guilt is touched on once by employing a Shakespearean quotation. "The fault, dear Brutus, is not in our stars, but in ourselves that we are underlings" (LDJ 152), James Tyrone sighs—not, however, recognizing his own fault. His quotations are ridiculed by his sons; as Raleigh has remarked, in O'Neill's last plays we "are asked to take nothing on faith."[17] Tyrone's confidential disclosure of his failure is accepted as truth by Edmund and by the audience; yet its impact is lessened by the sneering Jamie a few minutes later: "He's been putting on the old sob act for you, eh?" (LDJ 157). And the ultimate question of guilt is left unsolved in this relativistic play: "Nothing is to blame except everybody."[18] Fate, fog, life itself, all of us may be guilty—yet finding a scapegoat does not change at all our unredeemable situation.

Act IV in *Long Day's Journey into Night* is magnificent;[19] and the quotations help to make it so. Each of the four Tyrones is driven to his final confession in a modified monologue. Everything said or done in the play contributes to these revelation scenes,[20] following one another in a series of scenic images. . . . Tyrone speaks of the ambitions of a young Shakespearean actor; and we realize, as Waith has acutely observed, "that his longing for his youth is no less poignant than his wife's."[21] If ever

[16]Sigvard Mårtensson, *Eugene O'Neills dramatik* (1957), pp. 118–19.

[17]Raleigh, p. 204.

[18]Raleigh, p. 95: a quotation from his own earlier study, "O'Neill's *Long Day's Journey into Night* and New England Irish-Catholicism," Gassner (ed.), *O'Neill*, p. 125. To Gassner, *Long Day's Journey* is "perhaps the modern theater's outstanding dramatization of the ambivalences omnipresent in the human species" *(Eugene O'Neill*, p. 40).

[19]". . . the fourth act is among the most powerful scenes in all dramatic literature" (Brustein, p. 350).

[20]"Dramatic exposition . . . finally became in effect the entire substance of the play itself," Raleigh concludes (p. 195). At the end of "the backward journey into the past," there are "the ultimate disclosures," "either confessionals or justifications" or a combination of these two modes (p. 197).

[21]Waith, "An Exercise in Unmasking," p. 190.

the life of a human being has been weighed on the stage, in a manner both honest and warm, if ever deep tragedy is in the next moment followed by tragi-comedy, this is the case.[22]

Edmund describes his experience of freedom and belonging on the sea. The passage is written in the same vein as the vision of Stephen Daedalus at the end of *A Portrait of the Artist as a Young Man.* "For a second you see—and seeing the secret, are the secret. For a second there is meaning!"—is not this what so many creative artists have experienced?[23] The epiphany is presented as momentary, it is a part of a tragedy that certainly does not sing in rapture for the ecstasy of living; and it is followed, as many of Edmund's and Jamie's speeches are, by a self-ironic afterthought. "It was a great mistake," Edmund grins wryly, "my being born a man, I would have been much more successful as a sea gull or a fish" (LDJ 153). And he agrees with his father that he has perhaps only the makings of a poet: "I just stammered. That's the best I'll ever do. I mean, if I live. Well, it will be faithful realism, at least. Stammering is the native eloquence of us fog people" (LDJ 154).

This is only the second climax in the act: Jamie is still to be revealed, and the final synthesis of the family situation is still to be achieved by letting Mary join the others. So is a focusing synthesis of several scenic means of expression to come. Behind the mask of the brother and best friend who has "put Edmund wise" on women and the world in general there has been jealousy and resentment in Jamie: he hates and loves his brother—and his mother. His "love" meeting with Fat Violet in the town brothel is a grotesque revenge on Mary; he brought Violet upstairs— where Mary is in the Tyrone house. When remembering Mary's first fall, he identifies his mother with the whores: "Christ, I'd never dreamed before that any women but whores took dope!" (LDJ 163). Jamie is partly dead—he is destructive and poisonous—while Edmund feels that he belongs to Life itself. This time there is a contrast, not an equation, as between Mary

[22]The universality of the characters is indicated by several critics: "these people become larger than their own small lives; they become humanity, looking for something but not knowing exactly what it is looking for" (John Chapman, in Miller's *Playwright's Progress,* p. 134: reprinted from the *New York Daily News,* Nov. 8, 1956). Cf. Chiari, *Landmarks of Contemporary Drama,* p. 139, and Braem, *Eugene O'Neill,* p. 120.

[23]Raleigh calls Edmund's modified monologue a "fumbling expression to what, so far, has been the climactic experience in American literature, what can only be called the American metaphysical ecstasy: man alone confronting a gigantic, looming feature of Nature" (p. 283).

and Tyrone: Edmund is called by Waith a "creator."[24] Yet there
is also love, of a helpless and moving kind, in Jamie: "Greater
love hath no man than this, that he saveth his brother from himself" (LDJ 167).[25]

The long day's journey into four monologues is completed,
and everything is revealed, when Mary comes down and plays the
piano "with a forgetful, stiff-fingered groping, as if an awkward
schoolgirl were practicing . . . for the first time" (LDJ 169-70).
Then she enters the final scenic image in the play. . . . It looks
for a while as if Edmund may break through her defenses; but
only for a while. She soon returns into her fog, listens but does
not hear Jamie quoting Swinburne (perfectly appropriately in this
context), and says her curtain line from far away in her past.[26]

According to certain formulas of critical thought, *Long
Day's Journey into Night* should be a poor play. It is "undoubtedly too long—one long scene seems almost irrelevant; there is
too much quoting of classic poetry; and the deliberate formless-
ness of it all is enervating. Still, it is a dramatic achievement of the
first order," "a masterpiece."[27] A euphemistic way of putting it
is to say that the play is great "in spite of"[28]—and then let the
merits remain largely unanalyzed.

If a play is a masterpiece "in spite of" several critical presuppositions, it is high time to start asking whether there is anything wrong—with the presuppositions. If we have not given up
the hope of finding rational explanations to art, we should be busy
looking for reasons *why Long Day's Journey into Night* is a
masterpiece—instead of weighing down the other end of the scale
with our inapplicable criteria. One thing is certain: emotional
power does not come through on the stage without some kind of

[24]Waith, p. 191.

[25]Carpenter finds in the scene between Edmund and Jamie "the true climax of
the play. It provides the final moment of illumination, and of tragic catharsis,"
because there is a conflict implied between Jamie's "mephistophelian cynicism
and Edmund's genuine tragic idealism" (pp. 161–62).

[26]To Raleigh, this scenic image is "the soul-chilling climax of the greatest
tragedy in the history of the American theater and one of the greatest tragedies of
the Western theater" (p. 238); to Brustein, Mary's final speech means O'Neill's
emergence from the night into the daylight—"into a perception of his true role as a
man and an artist" (p. 358).

[27]Bowen, *The Curse of the Misbegotten,* pp. 273, 366.

[28]In *O'Neill and the American Critic,* Miller goes as far as to say that O'Neill's
late plays will survive "in spite of, and not because of, the technical contributions
of these or any other of his plays" (p. 30).

technique; only physical power might. And *Long Day's Journey into Night* does not shout; it speaks through its form.

Admitting that the play is void of outer action, there is good reason to emphasize that it is full of inner action. It is within the speeches that a major part of the drama is acted; it is within the utterances that the masks are changed. O'Neill let himself be bound by the tradition of realism because he knew that he could utilize the amount of freedom granted to him by the shortish chain of this style. He was convinced of his ability to dance in these chains. He knew that he could write in a style infiltrated by the results of his experimental period; he knew how to achieve porousness by making every detail both realistic and symbolic. "His contrapuntal arrangement of events that are seen in the theatre and reported events, which become real in the theatre of the mind only, makes his realism a free and spacious style,"[29] Stamm writes, recognizing clearly an important aspect of O'Neill's dynamic realism. Yet the reminiscent speeches of *Long Day's Journey into Night* would be static if O'Neill had not employed his small circles, drawn to touch love and hatred, sympathy and antagonism, guilt and accusations. O'Neill does not only move backwards in time, he also makes the past present. The past is an actual phenomenon, not asking but demanding reactions from the agonized characters. The wild fluctuation in the mind of Caligula or Ponce de Leon was attached only to the stage situation; now O'Neill has also the rich orchestra of human memories to play with.

"The past is the present, isn't it? It's the future, too. We all try to lie out of that but life won't let us" (LDJ 87), Mary complains in one of her most lucid moments.[30] If the first sentence could be taken as the motto for O'Neill's technique, the second reveals the core of his tragic vision. In fact, this is a statement in which O'Neill's method of constructing his play and his vision meet one another. The circle had been his favorite structural formula ever since his early efforts: yet as late as in this confessional play we see how deeply it was rooted in his personal attitude toward life. Fate is in the circles, in the inescapable repetitions, in the power of the past over the present and over the

---

[29]Stamm, "'Faithful Realism,'" p. 249.

[30]"Hating the present, fearing the future, he withdraws into the past, and writes his plays on the theme of time and memory," Brustein writes about all existential tragedians (p. 30).

future.[31] It may shout with the foghorn, too—but the sound has a meaning only to those who are living through the long chain of small, inescapable circles. This is O'Neill's modern artistic approximation to Fate, more personal than his psychological one in *Mourning Becomes Electra*.

The basic motivation for the numerous repetitions in *Long Day's Journey into Night* is given above. Facing the paradox of length once again, we might formulate a question: how many links can one take out of a chain and still make it reach? The more links that are added to a chain, the longer and weightier it becomes; and to those who prefer chains of a smaller caliber, all that can be said is that these are the shackles given to his characters by a tragedian. Some of the repetitions are further motivated by an urge to render ironically conflicting versions of familiar stories at different points of the action and by different characters: Tyrone's picture of Mary's father deviates from that cherished by Mary herself; Mary speaks of her falling in love in contrasting ways.[32] If after these considerations there is still a temptation to abridge, let it happen in small bits, mostly somewhere in the first three acts. It certainly will not do to say in an offhand manner that "there is too much quoting of classic poetry" or that a whole scene is irrelevant.

Long Day's Journey into Night is seen by Mottram as a synthesis of O'Neill's playwriting career. His "earliest one-acters melt into Edmund's sea-voyaging region of dream reality"; there is material from the saloons, utilized even in a group of other plays; *The Straw* is represented by Edmund's tuberculosis; "the Strindbergian elemental family is at last achieved without bogus classicism or pop-Freudianism"; and "the calm of *The Iceman Cometh* comes through again in this last harbour."[33] It is possible to speak of a synthesis from another point of view as well: O'Neill applies here several scenic means of expression he

---

[31]"The vicious circle becomes obsessive. The action lasts for one day, but it might have lasted for a century: it lasts in fact as long as the torments of hell" (Nicola Chiaromonte, "Eugene O'Neill," *Sewanee Review, 68,* 1960, 496). Raleigh remarks that O'Neill, Joyce, and Proust all based their major works "on their own memories," thus exercising a kind of "self-directed psychoanalysis" (p. 83).

[32]"One of the great sources of power of *Long Day's Journey* arises from the fact that four passionate but disparate imaginations are all focused on essentially the same set of past facts. But how differently this identical past comes out of each of the four wells of memory!" (Raleigh, p. 204).

[33]Mottram, "Men and Gods," p. 43.

knows thoroughly from previous usages. There is the idea of the fog, expressed mainly through a repetitive sound effect; there are modified monologues, again as the climaxes of the play; there is a continuous circular movement in the dialogue; symbolic significance gradually gathers around one portion of the setting; there are quotations rendering an additional layer of meaning. In a way, the quotations are still another modification of masks: by reciting a poem it is possible for the characters to express feelings not otherwise revealed.

All these means of expression are used in a purposeful way and executed flawlessly within the limits of the style chosen by the playwright: dynamic realism. Even in a play with little or no plot there can be quite a lot of interaction between the scenic images. Besides, *Long Day's Journey into Night* has a plot of an unconventional kind: its action proceeds through the fog into the monologues. Agreeing with Gassner in that "a continuing tension between naturalism and a variety of alternatives of dramatic stylization has characterized the century's theatre,"[34] we might call *Long Day's Journey into Night* one of O'Neill's major answers to the challenge created by this tension. It is more than a major answer: it is a masterful one.

[34]Gassner, *Theatre at the Crossroads*, p. xiv.

Egil Törnqvist

Parallel Characters and Situations in
Long Day's Journey into Night

PARALLEL CHARACTERS

In a tightly composed, structurally conventional play like *Journey,* we find several parallel characters appearing only in the dialogue. Thus, during the long talk between Edmund and Tyrone in the final act both cannot help drawing attention to painful parallel cases. "Booze and consumption" killed Dowson (135) and Mary's father (137)—as it may Edmund. And Dante Gabriel Rossetti "was a dope fiend" (135)—like Mary. The very things that should not be mentioned *are* mentioned, because the characters cannot get away from themselves; even when talking about other things, they keep thinking about their own fate; and the slips are illustrations of their spiritual isolation; in a minor figure they parallel the more serious blows the Tyrones deal to one another, for rightly considered these too are slips, illustrative of their inability to transcend their isolation and their past. These parallels, together with others (the suicide of Tyrone's grandfather as compared to the suicide attempts of Edmund and Mary; Cathleen's uncle, who drank himself to death as Jamie doubtless will do), provide a dark, fateful backdrop for the drama of the Tyrones and widen its scope; they turn, as it were, the domestic drama into a universal tragedy.

Other parallels, more amply dealt with in the play, have meanings beyond this basic one. Here again we are confronted with figures symbolizing tendencies within the pivotal character, Mary Tyrone. There is, for example, the somewhat surprising resemblance between Mary and Fat Violet, the prostitute at whose breast Jamie seeks consolation. The obvious and glaring contrast between Violet and Mary, the whore and the "virgin," the woman of all men and the woman of no man (for this is what Mary's name and dream of becoming a nun amount to), is leveled

From *Egil Törnqvist,* A Drama of Souls: Studies in O'Neill's Supernaturalistic Technique, *1969. Reprinted by permission of Yale University Press.*

out by a more basic similarity.[1] Thus, in her first speech Mary points out that she has "gotten too fat" (14), and it is pointed out that Jamie likes fat women (134, 160) but that he finds Violet too fat (160). Both women play the piano. Violet has been "on drunks" lately (159), as Mary has relapsed into morphinism; and Jamie brings the two together in his remark that before he discovered his mother's addiction, he could not imagine "that any women but whores took dope" (163); in a sense, his mother thus appears as a whore to him; by not loving him enough, by hiding in her dope world, she betrays him, makes him forever hunger for love. Yet Mary too hungers for love; and so does Violet. Both feel lonely, unpopular; Mary lacks friends; customers do not fall for Vi. Both hope to be loved despite their deformities, Violet despite her fatness, Mary despite her deficiencies as a wife and mother. As soon as Jamie knows that the beloved mother has left him forever, he goes to sleep with Violet. He believes that he selects her out of consideration for a fellow bum. What he does not see is that his concern for Violet is motivated by her resemblance to Mary, that she functions as an admittedly unsuccessful mother substitute. Thus Jamie's visit to Mamie Burns' brothel becomes a pathetic illustration of his inability to get away from the mother; his love will follow her still.

Even closer is the parallel between Mary and Bridget, the cook.[2] The fog affects Bridget's rheumatism as it does Mary's (41, 99). And she appears to be as much of a whiskey addict as Mary is a "dope fiend." Their desperation, made acute—or rather symbolized—by their bodily pain, stems, as in the case of Violet, from an intense feeling of loneliness. In Act I Bridget, who needs company, keeps Mary in the kitchen for a long while with "lies about her relations" (102). In Act II Mary keeps Cathleen in the living room with memories of her own happy past which, according to Tyrone, must be taken "with a grain of salt" (137). She too needs a listener.

Cathleen describes Bridget as little better than a maniac, who cannot stand being left alone.

. . . she's like a raging divil. She'll bite my head off (99).

---

[1] Mary Ellen, the names of O'Neill's mother, is actually the term for an amateur prostitute; as the Gelbs indicate (p. 167), O'Neill was familiar with this expression.

[2] It is interesting to note that Mary Ellen's mother—O'Neill's grandmother—was named Bridget (Gelb, p. 12).

> If she don't get something to quiet her temper, she'll be after me
> with a cleaver (106).

If we are reminded here of Ella Harris in *Chillun,* the association
is apt, for Ella, like Mary, seems modeled to a great extent on
O'Neill's mother. Hence Bridget, being another Ella, is seen to
be another Mary. Never appearing but always (since we are constantly reminded of her presence in the dialogue and in the exits
to the kitchen) lurking in the background, she comes to personify
the reckless, destructive impulse within Mary, which finally
"kills" her three men. Mary says:

> It's no use finding fault with Bridget. She doesn't listen. I can't
> threaten her, or she'd threaten she'd leave. And she does do her
> best at times. It's too bad they seem to be just the times you're sure
> to be late, James. Well, there's this consolation: it's difficult to tell
> from her cooking whether she's doing her best or her worst (71 f.).

This is no doubt a disguised self-portrait and a speech of defense.
In her marriage Mary claims to have "done the best [she]
could—under the circumstances" (114). She is no more suited for
it than Bridget is for cooking. And besides, Tyrone has never given
her much of a chance; he has never really understood that just as
you cannot expect the food to taste good if you are late for it, so
you can't expect a woman to be a good wife unless you give her a
proper environment, which she can delight in. Such is Mary's
defensive view; hidden beneath it is her other, more deeply felt
view that she is herself to blame. It is precisely because she feels
so guilty that Mary cannot accept any blame; she refutes it, like
Bridget, by not listening and by eventually "leaving" her family.

PARALLEL SITUATIONS

In *Journey* O'Neill has inserted what to a casual observer
may seem a digression out of tune with the serious mood of the
play and completely unrelated to it. I refer to the Harker-
Shaughnessy episode, which fascinated O'Neill to the extent that
he used it again and more extensively in *Misbegotten.*

Shaughnessy is a poor Irish tenant on a farm owned by
Tyrone. This farm borders on the estate belonging to Harker, a
Yankee Standard Oil millionaire. Edmund has just met
Shaughnessy and he is reporting what the tenant has told him:

(grins at his father provocatively) Well, you remember, Papa, the ice pond on Harker's estate is right next to the farm, and you remember Shaughnessy keeps pigs. Well, it seems there's a break in the fence and the pigs have been bathing in the millionaire's ice pond, and Harker's foreman told him he was sure Shaughnessy had broken the fence on purpose to give his pigs a free wallow (23).

But when Harker came to rebuke Shaughnessy, the Irishman

accused Harker of making his foreman break down the fence to entice the pigs into the ice pond in order to destroy them. The poor pigs, Shaughnessy yelled, had caught their death of cold. Many of them were dying of pneumonia, and several others had been taken down with cholera from drinking the poisoned water (24).

This anecdote obviously helps to characterize the Tyrones in the sense that their reactions to it reveal something about their natures. Tyrone's reaction is especially illuminating; while he spontaneously sides with Shaughnessy, he gives some half-hearted support to Harker. But the story is also, I would suggest, the story of the Tyrone family in disguise. Thus the poor farm bordering on the rich estate illustrates Tyrone's transition from poverty to wealth. It is clear that he shares characteristics with both combatants—hence his divided sympathies. He is of humble Irish origin like Shaughnessy, who nevertheless claims that he would be a "King of Ireland" (24), if he had his rights, a claim that would not be foreign to Tyrone, judging by his name (Törnqvist, 1966, p. 372) and pride in the old country. Like Harker, he is a well-to-do "businessman" and landowner; Harker is ironically referred to as a "king of America" (23), and Tyrone has acquired a similar position as a nation-wide matinée idol.[3] While accumulating his wealth and rising in society Tyrone has declined from "King" to "king," from Ireland to America, from Shakespeare to Monte Cristo, from artist to businessman. Like the pigs, he has run away from the poor farm to the rich estate, but in the process he has fatally poisoned himself. Mary too has moved outside her fenced-in, innocent childhood environment with the same result. Both of them find that they can no longer call their souls their own.

[3]According to the Gelbs (p. 220) James O'Neill was worth between $100,000 and $200,000 in cash and real estate around 1912. Much earlier, in 1882, he had been the actor-manager of a play called *The American King* (Alexander, 1962, p. 51). Beginning with this play of little merit, James gave up his artistic demands and began to look at plays from a business point of view (cf. *Journey*, 149 f.).

Many of the pigs, we learn, die of pneumonia after they have caught cold. Edmund is, for a long time, thought to suffer from a summer cold—until it is disclosed that he is affected by a far more fatal disease: consumption.[4] Other pigs die from drinking the poisoned ice water. Tyrone's father died by, perhaps deliberately, mistaking "rat poison for flour" (147).[5] Tyrone himself early began poisoning his sons by giving them whiskey as medicine, thereby laying a foundation for future alcoholism. During the long day we actually see the three men "wallow" in whiskey and ice water to make life bearable and short. Mary was poisoned by the quack who first gave her morphine; Tyrone constantly refers to the morphine as "the poison" (78, 111, 123, 139, 142, 174). Jamie jealously "poisoned" Eugene with measles (from which the baby died) and Edmund with "worldly wisdom"—hard drinking and Broadway tarts—when he was merely a boy (34).

Although it is never made completely clear, it is strongly implied that it was Shaughnessy who broke down the fence. Poor as he is, he wants to give his pigs "a free wallow" at the expense of the hated Yankee millionaire; thus we may construe his motives. But the cheap bath has, as we have seen, consequences unforeseen by the tenant. In the same way Tyrone, unable to unlearn his childhood lesson of "the value of a dollar," tries to get everything second hand and as a result works destruction on his family. It was the cheap quack he sent Mary to that got her started on morphine. And it is a cheap sanatorium, "endowed by a group of millionaire factory owners, for the benefit of their workers" (149), to which he finally decides to send Edmund; and the son evidently stands as slim a chance of survival there as do the pigs in Harker's ice pond. The choice the-poor-Irish-boy-in-Tyrone makes is the choice Shaughnessy would have made; it is motivated not merely by an excessive money consciousness but also by a wish to benefit, for once, from the plutocrats, who had treated Tyrone and his family as little better than slaves; Tyrone's sanatorium plan is thus in a sense another battle fought against the Yankees.

Shaughnessy's violent attack on Harker, blaming him for what he himself has most likely done, may be seen as a grotesque and simplified version of the way each of the Tyrones reacts with regard to the major "crimes" committed in the past. It is precisely when they feel most guilty that they blame others, applying Shaughnessy's technique of attacking before being attacked; he

---

[4] According to the death verdict, Jamie died of pneumonia (Gelb, p. 532).
[5] It may be noted that "rat poison" is a term for bad liquor in *Iceman* (619).

who evokes their guilt-feelings immediately turns into an enemy against whom they must defend themselves; their attacks thus stem primarily from a need to relieve themselves from an acute self-hatred.

Yet the fact that the question "Who broke down the fence that opened the way for the pigs' destruction?" is not unequivocally answered is of some significance. No doubt O'Neill was unwilling to provide a clear answer because he was aware that the question foreshadows the much larger one we ask ourselves at the end of the play: "Who is to blame for the destruction of the Tyrone family?" The whole play, in a sense, is devoted to answering this question. The web of guilt is so complex, is distributed to so many hands and stretches so far back in time that, although we realize that all the Tyrones have their share in it, and Tyrone perhaps most of all, we are ultimately left with Mary's philosophy that life, rather than any one of them, must carry the heaviest responsibility.

Structurally, the pig story springs naturally from the form chosen by O'Neill for his play. The technique of gradual revelation strictly adhered to in *Journey* prevents overt references to the family fate in the early acts; the play structure itself is designed as a long journey into the dark interior of the family and its individual members. The dramatist is obviously presented with a problem here. For the sake of dramatic suspense he is forced to make his characters withhold important information, while for the sake of structural unity he is forced to make them deliver it. He must therefore make the dialogue in the early acts function on (at least) two levels. Even if we do not—and, in fact, often cannot—grasp its more profound meaning at a first reading/hearing, we frequently sense that what the characters are saying is of a greater significance than it appears to be at the moment when it is presented; and we axiomatically assume that some of it will be made clear in the process of the play. This awareness of as of yet unintelligible levels creates a feeling of suspense, which piques our interest before it has been stirred by the human drama before us.

The parallel includes a marked contrast in *tone* between the anecdote and the ensuing action, which illustrates its meaning. The Tyrones can laugh at the Shaughnessy episode precisely because they do not realize that it is their own story in disguise. Had it been told at the end of the long day they—and we—would doubtless view it differently. Thus, by changing the perspective, O'Neill illustrates how life, depending on our degree of involvement, can be seen either as a farce or as a tragedy.

Eric Bentley

Eugene O'Neill's Pietà

Back to the farm. The New England farm of *Desire Under the Elms* and *Beyond the Horizon*. The issue is ownership. The villain of the piece tries to wrest it from the heroine and her father. He even gets the hero on his side. So heroine and father plot our hero's ruin: he is to be disgraced by being found in our heroine's bed. I am telling the story of Eugene O'Neill's *A Moon for the Misbegotten,*[1] and have come to the end of the second act. In Act Three comes a surprise. Our heroine has the opportunity of carrying out her revenge but she discovers that our hero is not on the villain's side after all, has not betrayed her. The occasion turns into a moonlit love scene, poetic and bedless. In Act Four, a second surprise follows. The heroine's father does not arrive with gun and witnesses as he had promised. We find he had known our hero's probity all along. He wanted to get the young couple into bed and couldn't think of a less unusual way to manage it. He knew heroes marry the girls they make love to, and he wanted to trap our hero into marriage. The play doesn't end with marriage, though. It ends with the heroine's wishing the hero an early, if painless, death. It doesn't have a happy ending, it has a happy middle. It is built round—written for the sake of—its third act, in which we see our hero as "a damned soul coming . . . in the moonlight to confess and be forgiven and find peace for a night."

A well-made melodrama in which the expectations of melodrama are deliberately disappointed: Bernard Shaw has familiarized us with the pattern and convinced us that the disappointment may be more apparent and formal than substantial and real. And O'Neill touches upon the central substances and realities of modern life and drama. In his preoccupation with death-in-life—modern man a living corpse—he reminds us of Ib-

---

[1] Destined to be the last play O'Neill published. Still unproduced in New York (Summer, 1954).

sen. Like Strindberg, he shows people torturing each other with words; like Pirandello, he shows them torturing *themselves* with words. Stylistically, there is a kinship with O'Casey: especially in his climactic third act he attempts to transfigure his naturalistic prose into high poetry. And in stating his main theme—guilt—he seeks to place his play in the main stream of modern literature. (In the theater its popularity, like that of *The Cocktail Party,* would depend on the degree to which it arouses and appeases the public's sense of guilt.)

Perhaps I've already made it apparent how close *A Moon for the Misbegotten* is to other work by O'Neill himself. It is closest to the last play he published, *The Iceman Cometh,* not only in style and lay-out but in having at its core a confession of guilt from a man who has wronged a woman. The "inner" climax which O'Neill substitutes for the expected melodramatic climax is his hero's confession that he was drunk when his dying mother last set eyes on him and that he slept with a whore in the train that carried his mother's corpse. Second to *The Iceman Cometh,* the most obvious and significant tie is with *Anna Christie.* In all three plays drinking and whoring are presented as the principal human pursuits, while above all three there hover the ideas of virginity and motherhood, associated in every case with Catholicism and Ireland.

Why not? The material is magnificent. If it appears ridiculous in O'Neill's plays it is because he has not succeeded in molding it. That his language, for example, is unequal to the tasks he assigns to it is generally admitted, though his admirers shrug the fact off with the observation that you can't blame him for not being Shakespeare. One might, however, expect so ambitious a writer to stand comparison with our more talented novelists. O'Neill has attempted the poetry of colloquial American speech, the poetry of the underworld, yet has never written a page to compare with *The Killers* or *A Clean, Well Lighted Place.* The tough talk of *A Moon for the Misbegotten* may be closer to the talk of 1923 (the date of the action) than I am equipped to say but anyone can see that the words have less vitality than even the worst of Hemingway. (Assignment for a linguist: how much of O'Neill's dialect and slang comes from life, how much from stage tradition and personal hunch?) Style is meaning. Hemingway's style has often succeeded in reaching in a few lines much the same sort of pessimism that O'Neill will circumnavigate for hundreds of pages.

What Europeans call the "American" style—i.e. the

"tough" style—operates chiefly as an ironical mask for sensitivity. Undoubtedly O'Neill realized—with his brain, that is—how much of American life there is in this contrast. The hero of *A Moon for the Misbegotten* "only acts [and, we may add, talks] like he's hard and shameless to get back at life when it's tormenting him—and who doesn't?" Unhappily, O'Neill himself shows that embarrassment in the face of life, that shame in the presence of the spirit, which is the source of the "American" way of talking. He is afraid to have anyone mention sin without having them add "Nuts with that sin bunk" or to quote a poem without at once denouncing "the old poetic bull."

The prime symptom—or perhaps prime cause—of this embarrassment is fear of sex—fear of woman as woman, longing for her as mother or as virgin. There was a moment (that of *Days without End*) when O'Neill seemed to have settled for the Virgin Mother, like his Irish antecedents. In *A Moon for the Misbegotten,* he finds an equivalent in the terms of his own naturalistic mysticism, describing his heroine as "a virgin who bears a dead child in the night," and adding: "the dawn finds her still a virgin." The grandiosity here is that of adolescent poetry: corny words for corny conceptions. The heroine of *A Moon for the Misbegotten* is 5′ 11″ tall (to the hero's 5′ 9″) and weighs a hundred and eighty pounds. On the side of the comical-grotesque such a phenomenon has possibilities which are partly realized in one bravura scene in which she and her father bawl the villain out. Beyond that we inescapably have the impression of neurotic fantasy unorganized into art. In place of organization, clichés and formulae: Anna Christie was the whore with the heart of a virgin, this new heroine is the virgin-who-seems-to-be-a-whore-till-the-truth-comes-out. (Assignment for a director: cast this part. Having done so, cast the same actress in any other play.)

A Moon for the Misbegotten will change no one's opinion of Eugene O'Neill. It is neither his worst work nor his best. If it is more serious, and in some ways more meritorious, than most recent plays, so much the worse for most recent plays. I rather think its central image—that of a giant virgin holding in her arms a dipsomaniac lecher with a heart of gold—may stand in all minds as O'Neill's monument; for admirers will find it characteristic in grandeur and poetry, while others will find in it, clinically speaking, neurotic fantasy indulged rather than exploited and, critically speaking, poetry strained after rather than achieved.

Selected Bibliography

PRIMARY SOURCES

Plays in Order of First Publication

Published by Gorham Press, Boston:
>	*Thirst and Other One-Act Plays,* 1914. Includes: "Thirst," "The Web," "Warnings," "Fog," "Recklessness."

Published by Boni and Liveright, New York:
>	*The Moon of the Caribbees and Six Other Plays of the Sea,* 1919. Includes: "Moon of the Caribbees," "Bound East for Cardiff," "The Long Voyage Home," "In the Zone," "Ile," "Where the Cross Is Made," "The Rope."

>	*Beyond the Horizon,* 1920.

>	*The Emperor Jones, Diff'rent, The Straw,* 1921.

>	*Gold,* 1921.

>	*The Hairy Ape, Anna Christie, The First Man,* 1922.

>	*All God's Chillun Got Wings, Welded,* 1924.

>	*Desire under the Elms,* 1925.

>	*The Great God Brown, The Fountain, The Moon of the Caribbees,* and other plays, 1926.

>	*Marco Millions,* 1927.

>	*Lazarus Laughed,* 1927.

>	*Strange Interlude,* 1928.

Published by Horace Liveright, New York:
>	*Dynamo,* 1929.

>	*Mourning Becomes Electra,* 1931.

Published by Random House, New York:
>	*Ah, Wilderness!* 1933.

>	*Days without End,* 1934.

>	*The Iceman Cometh,* 1946.

>	*A Moon for the Misbegotten,* 1952.

Published by the Yale University Press, New Haven, Conn.:
>	*Long Day's Journey into Night,* 1956.

>	*A Touch of the Poet,* 1957.

>	*Hughie,* 1959.

>	*More Stately Mansions,* 1964.

Collections of O'Neill's Plays.

The Complete Works of Eugene O'Neill, 2 vols. New York: Boni and Liveright, 1924–1925.

Nine Plays by Eugene O'Neill, selected by the author, introduction by Joseph Wood Krutch. New York: Horace Liveright, 1932. Republished as a Modern Library Giant. New York: Random House, n.d.

The Plays of Eugene O'Neill, Wilderness edition, 12 vols. New York: Charles Scribner's, 1934–1935. Includes notes by the author.

The Plays of Eugene O'Neill, 3 vols. New York: Random House, 1951. The standard edition for plays published before 1951.

Ten "Lost" Plays of Eugene O'Neill. New York: Random House, 1964. Includes: "Thirst," "The Web," "Warnings," "Fog," "Recklessness," "Abortion," "The Movie Man," "The Sniper," "A Wife for a Life," *Servitude.*

Current Paperback Editions of O'Neill's Plays

Seven Plays of the Sea by Eugene O'Neill. New York: Vintage Books. Includes: "The Long Voyage Home," "The Moon of the Caribbees," "Bound East for Cardiff," "In the Zone," "The Rope," "Ile," "Where the Cross Is Made."

Six Short Plays of Eugene O'Neill. New York: Vintage Books. Includes: "Before Breakfast," "The Dreaming Kid," *The Straw, Gold, Diff'rent, Welded.*

Three Plays of Eugene O'Neill. New York: Vintage Books. Includes: *Desire under the Elms, Strange Interlude, Mourning Becomes Electra.*

The Emperor Jones, Anna Christie, The Hairy Ape. New York: Vintage Books.

The Iceman Cometh. New York: Vintage Books.

A Moon for the Misbegotten. New York: Vintage Books.

The Later Plays of Eugene O'Neill. New York: Modern Library College Editions. Includes: *Ah, Wilderness!, A Touch of the Poet, Hughie, A Moon for the Misbegotten.*

Long Day's Journey into Night. New Haven, Conn.: Yale Paperbound.

A Touch of the Poet. New Haven, Conn.: Yale Paperbound.

Hughie. New Haven, Conn.: Yale Paperbound.

More Stately Mansions. New Haven, Conn.: Yale Paperbound.

Some Important Critical Comments by O'Neill

"Strindberg and Our Theatre." Provincetown Playbill No. 1. Reproduced in Helen Deutsch and Stella Hanau, *The Provincetown: A Story of Our Theatre, 1915–1929*. New York: Farrar and Rinehart, 1931. Also in Cargill, Fagin, and Fisher, *O'Neill and His Plays* (see below), and Horst Frenz, ed., *American Playwrights on Drama*, New York: Hill and Wang, 1965.

"Memoranda on Masks," "Second Thoughts," and "A Dramatist's Notebook." Three essays on masks, first published in *The American Spectator* (November 1932, December 1932, January 1933). Reproduced in Cargill, Fagin, and Fisher, *O'Neill and His Plays* (see below).

Letter to Arthur Hobson Quinn on being "a bit of a poet, who has labored with the spoken word to evolve original rhythms of beauty where beauty apparently isn't . . . and to see the transfiguring nobility of tragedy, in as near the Greek sense as one can grasp it, in seemingly the most ignoble, debased lives." Printed in Arthur Hobson Quinn, *A History of the American Drama from the Civil War to the Present Day*, New York: Harper, 1927, vol. II, p. 199.

Letter on the "happy ending" of *Anna Christie, New York Times,* December 18, 1921. Reproduced in Quinn, op.cit., pp. 177–178.

O'Neill on *The Hairy Ape*. A group of O'Neill's comments on his play are reproduced in Richard Levin, ed., *Tragedy: Plays, Theory, and Criticism*, New York: Harcourt, Brace, 1960, pp. 129–130.

"The Playwright Explains" [on *The Great God Brown*], *New York Evening Post*, February 13, 1926. Reproduced in Quinn, op.cit., pp. 192–194. Also in Barrett H. Clark, *Eugene O'Neill: The Man and His Plays*, New York: Dover, 1947, pp. 104–106, and Walter J. Meserve, ed., *Discussions of Modern American Drama*, Boston: Heath, 1966, pp. 130–131.

Letter to George Jean Nathan on *Dynamo*. Quoted in George Jean Nathan, "The Theatre," *The American Mercury*, January 1929, p. 119. Also in Alan S. Downer, ed., *American Drama and Its Critics*, Chicago: University of Chicago Press, 1965, and Toronto: Gemini Books, 1965, p. 98.

"O'Neill's Own Story of *Electra* in the Making," *New York Herald Tribune*, November 8, 1931. Reproduced as "Working Notes and Extracts from a Fragmentary Work Diary" in Barrett H. Clark, ed., *European Theories of the Drama, with a Supple-*

ment on the American Drama, New York: Crown, 1947, pp. 529–536. Also in Horst Frenz, ed., *American Playwrights on Drama,* op.cit., pp. 3–15.

SECONDARY SOURCES

Bibliographies and Concordance

Atkinson, Jennifer McCabe. *Eugene O'Neill: A Descriptive Bibliography.* Pittsburgh: University of Pittsburgh Press, 1974.
Bryer, Jackson, *The Merrill Checklist of Eugene O'Neill.* Columbus, Ohio: Merrill, 1971.
Miller, Jordan Y. *Eugene O'Neill and the American Critic: A Summary and Bibliographical Checklist.* Hamden, Conn.: Archon Books, 1962. Second ed. revised, 1973.
Reaver, J. Russell. *An O'Neill Concordance.* 3 vols. Detroit: Gale, 1969.
Salem, James M. "Eugene O'Neill," *A Guide to Critical Reviews—Part 1: American Drama, 1909–1969. 2nd ed.* Metuchen, N.J.: Scarecrow Press, 1973, pp. 348–372.
Sanborn, Ralph, and Barrett H. Clark. *A Bibliography of the Works of Eugene O'Neill Together with the Collected Poems of Eugene O'Neill.* New York: B. Blom, 1965.

Books on O'Neill

I   Mainly biographical:

Alexander, Doris. *The Tempering of Eugene O'Neill.* New York: Harcourt, Brace & World, 1962.
Boulton, Agnes. *Part of a Long Story.* New York: Doubleday, 1958.
Bowen, Croswell, with the assistance of Shane O'Neill. *The Curse of the Misbegotten: A Tale of the House of O'Neill.* New York: McGraw-Hill, 1959.
Clark, Barrett H. *Eugene O'Neill: The Man and His Plays.* New York: Dover, 1947. [Revised ed. of *Eugene O'Neill,* 1926].
Gelb, Arthur and Barbara. *O'Neill.* New York: Harper & Row, 1962. A major biographical work.
Sheaffer, Louis. *O'Neill: Son and Playwright.* Boston: Little, Brown, 1968. With the following volume, a major biography.
———. *O'Neill: Son and Artist.* Boston: Little, Brown, 1973.

II Mainly critical:

Bogard, Travis. *Contour in Time: The Plays of Eugene O'Neill.* New York: Oxford, 1972.

Cargill, Oscar, N. Bryllion Fagin, and William J. Fisher, eds. *O'Neill and His Plays: Four Decades of Criticism.* New York: New York University Press, 1961.

Carpenter, Frederic I. *Eugene O'Neill.* New York: Twayne, 1964.

Engel, Edwin A. *The Haunted Heroes of Eugene O'Neill.* Cambridge: Harvard University Press, 1953.

Falk, Doris V. *Eugene O'Neill and the Tragic Tension: An Interpretative Study of the Plays.* New Brunswick, N.J.: Rutgers University Press, 1958.

Frazer, Winifred D. *Love as Death in* The Iceman Cometh: *A Modern Treatment of an Ancient Theme.* Gainesville: University of Florida Press, 1967.

Frenz, Horst. *Eugene O'Neill,* tr. Helen Sebba. New York: Frederick Ungar, 1971.

Gassner, John. *Eugene O'Neill.* Minneapolis: University of Minnesota Press, 1965.

————, ed. *O'Neill: A Collection of Critical Essays.* Englewood Cliffs, N.J.: Prentice-Hall, 1964.

Leech, Clifford. *Eugene O'Neill.* London: Oliver & Boyd, 1963. New York: Grove Press, 1963.

Long, Chester Clayton. *The Role of Nemesis in the Structure of Selected Plays by Eugene O'Neill.* The Hague: Mouton, 1968.

Miller, Jordan Y., ed. *Playwright's Progress: O'Neill and the Critics.* Chicago: Scott, Foresman, 1965.

Raleigh, John Henry, ed. The Iceman Cometh: *A Collection of Critical Essays.* Englewood Cliffs, N.J.: Prentice-Hall, 1968.

————. *The Plays of Eugene O'Neill.* Carbondale: Southern Illinois University Press, 1965. Also published as *Eugene O'Neill: The Man and His Works.* Toronto: Forum House, 1969.

Scheibler, Rolf. *The Late Plays of Eugene O'Neill.* Bern: Francke Verlag, 1970.

Skinner, Richard Dana. *Eugene O'Neill: A Poet's Quest.* New York: Longmans, Green, 1935. Revised ed. New York: Russell & Russell, 1964.

Tiusanen, Timo. *O'Neill's Scenic Images.* Princeton, N.J.: Princeton University Press, 1968.

Törnqvist, Egil. *A Drama of Souls: Studies in O'Neill's Super-naturalistic Technique.* New Haven, Conn.: Yale University Press, 1969.

Winther, Sophus Keith. *Eugene O'Neill: A Critical Study.* New York: Random House, 1934. Revised ed. New York: Russell & Russell, 1961.

Articles on O'Neill

It is emphasized that this list is necessarily only a part of the immense bibliography on O'Neill. The student of O'Neill should also bear in mind that almost every book on modern drama contains a passage, perhaps a chapter, devoted to O'Neill. A good survey of such chapters is given in the bibliographical essay "Eugene O'Neill" by John Henry Raleigh in *Sixteen Modern American Authors: A Survey of Research and Criticism,* ed. Jackson R. Bryer, Durham, N.C.: Duke University Press, 1974.

Alexander, Doris M. "Eugene O'Neill and *Light on the Path.*" *Modern Drama,* III (December 1960), 260–267.

———. "Eugene O'Neill as Social Critic." *American Quarterly,* VI (Winter 1954), 349–363.

———. "Hugo of *The Iceman Cometh:* Realism and O'Neill." *American Quarterly,* V (Winter 1953), 357–366.

———. "*Lazarus Laughed* and Buddha." *Modern Language Quarterly,* XVII (December 1956), 357–365.

———. "Psychological Fate in *Mourning Becomes Electra.*" *PMLA,* LXVIII (December 1953), 923–934.

———. "*Strange Interlude* and Schopenhauer." *American Literature,* XXV (May 1953), 213–228.

Andreach, Robert J. "O'Neill's Use of Dante in *The Fountain* and *The Hairy Ape.*" *Modern Drama,* X (May 1967), 48–56.

———. "O'Neill's Women in *The Iceman Cometh.*" *Renascence,* XVIII (Winter 1966), 89–98.

Arestad, Sverre. "*The Iceman Cometh* and *The Wild Duck.*" *Scandinavian Studies,* XX (February 1948), 1–11.

Asselineau, Roger. "*Desire under the Elms:* A Phase of O'Neill's Philosophy." *Festschrift Rudolf Stamm,* ed. Eduard Kolb und Jörg Hasler. Bern: Francke Verlag, 1969, 277–283.

———. "*Mourning Becomes Electra* As a Tragedy." *Modern Drama,* I (December 1958), 143–150.

Baum, Bernard. "*The Tempest* and *The Hairy Ape:* The Literary Incarnation of Mythos." *Modern Language Quarterly,* XIV (September 1953), 258–273.

Bentley, Eric. "Trying to Like O'Neill." *Kenyon Reivew,* XIV (Summer 1952), 476–492.

Berkelman, Robert. "O'Neill's Everyman." *South Atlantic Quarterly,* LVIII (Autumn 1959), 609–616.

Blackburn, Clara. "Continental Influences on Eugene O'Neill's Expressionistic Dramas." *American Literature,* XIII (May 1941), 109–133.

Bowling, Charis Crosse. "The Touch of Poetry: A Study of the Role of Poetry in Three O'Neill Plays." *College Language Association Journal,* XII (September 1968), 43–55.

Brashear, William R. "O'Neill and Shaw: The Play as Will and Idea." *Criticism,* VIII (Spring 1966), 155–169.

———. "O'Neill's Schopenhauer Interlude." *Criticism,* VI, (Summer 1964), 256–265.

———. "The Wisdom of Silenus in O'Neill's *Iceman." American Literature,* XXXVI (May 1964), 180–188.

Busch, C. Trent, and Orton A. Jones. "Immortality Enough: The Influence of Strindberg on the Expressionism of Eugene O'Neill." *Southern Speech Journal,* XXXIII (Winter 1967), 129–139.

Carpenter, Frederic I. "Eugene O'Neill, the Orient, and American Transcendentalism." *Transcendentalism and Its Legacy,* ed. Myron Simon and Thornton H. Parsons. Ann Arbor: University of Michigan Press, 1966, 204–214.

———. "The Romantic Tragedy of Eugene O'Neill." *College English,* VI (February 1945), 250–258.

Chabrowe, Leonard. "Dionysus in *The Iceman Cometh." Modern Drama,* IV (February 1962), 377–388.

Clark, Marden J. "Tragic Effect in *The Hairy Ape." Modern Drama,* X (February 1968), 372–382.

Cohn, Ruby. "Absurdity in English: Joyce and O'Neill." *Comparative Drama,* III (Fall 1969), 156–161.

Cole, Lester, and John Howard Lawson. "Two Views on O'Neill." *Masses and Mainstream,* VII (June 1954), 56–63.

Cunningham, Frank P. *"The Great God Brown* and O'Neill's Romantic Vision." *Ball State University Forum,* XIV (Summer 1973), 69–78.

Daiches, David. "Mourning Becomes O'Neill," *Encounter,* XVI (June 1961), 74–78.

Day, Cyrus. "Amor Fati: O'Neill's Lazarus as Superman and Savior." *Modern Drama,* III (December 1960), 297–305.

———. "The Iceman and the Bridegroom: Some Observations on the Death of O'Neill's Salesman." *Modern Drama,* I (May 1958), 3–9.

De Voto, Bernard. "Minority Report." *Saturday Review of Literature,* XV (November 21, 1936), 3–4, 16.

Dickinson, Hugh. "Eugene O'Neill: Fate as Form." *Drama Critique,* X (Spring 1967), 78–85.

Driver, Tom F. "On the Last Plays of Eugene O'Neill." *Tulane Drama Review,* III (December 1958), 8–20.

Engel, Edwin A. "Eugene O'Neill's Long Day's Journey into Light." *Michigan Alumnus Quarterly Review,* LXIII (Summer 1957), 348–354.

————. "Ideas in the Plays of Eugene O'Neill." *Ideas in the Drama: Selected Papers from the English Institute,* ed. John Gassner. New York: Columbia University Press, 1964, 101–124.

Falk, Doris V. "That Paradox, O'Neill." *Modern Drama,* VI (December 1963), 221–238.

Falk, Signi. "Dialogue in the Plays of Eugene O'Neill." *Modern Drama,* III (December 1960), 314–325.

Fergusson, Francis. "Eugene O'Neill." *Hound and Horn,* III (January–March 1930), 145–160.

Finkelstein, Sidney. "O'Neill's 'Long Day's Journey.' " *Mainstream,* XVI (June 1963), 47–51.

Fish, Charles. "Beginnings: O'Neill's *The Web." Princeton University Library Chronicle,* XXVII (Autumn 1965), 3–20.

Fitzgerald, John J. "The Bitter Harvest of O'Neill's Projected Cycle." *New England Quarterly,* XL (September 1967), 364–374.

————. "Guilt and Redemption in O'Neill's Last Play: A Study of *A Moon for the Misbegotten." Texas Quarterly,* IX (Spring 1966), 146–158.

Fleisher, Frederic. "Strindberg and O'Neill." *Symposium,* X (Spring 1956), 84–94.

Flory, Claude R. "Notes on the Antecedents of *Anna Christie." PMLA,* LXXXVI (January 1971), 77–83.

Frazer, Winifred L. "Chris and Poseidon: Man Versus God in *Anna Christie." Modern Drama,* XII (December 1969), 279–285.

————. "King Lear and Hickey: Bridegroom and Iceman." *Modern Drama,* XV (December 1972), 267–278.

Frenz, Horst. "Eugene O'Neill's *Desire under the Elms* and Henrik Ibsen's *Rosmersholm." Jahrbuch für Amerikastudien,* IX (1964), 160–165.

————, and Martin Mueller. "More Shakespeare and Less Aeschylus in Eugene O'Neill's *Mourning Becomes Electra.*" *American Literature,* XXXVIII (March 1966), 85–100.

Gillett, Peter J. "O'Neill and the Racial Myths." *Twentieth Century Literature,* XVIII (January–October 1972), 111–120.

Granger, Bruce I. "Illusion and Reality in Eugene O'Neill." *Modern Language Notes,* LXXIII (March 1958), 179–186.

Griffin, Ernest G. "Pity, Alienation and Reconciliation in Eugene O'Neill." *Mosaic,* II (Fall 1968), 66–76.

Gump, Margaret. "From Ape to Man and from Man to Ape." *Kentucky Foreign Language Quarterly,* IV (Fall 1957), 177–185.

Hartman, Murray. *"Desire under the Elms* in the Light of Strindberg's Influence." *American Literature,* XXXIII (November 1961), 360–369.

———. "The Skeletons in O'Neill's *Mansions.*" *Drama Survey,* V (Winter 1966–67), 276–279.

———. "Strindberg and O'Neill." *Educational Theatre Journal,* XVIII (October 1966), 216–223.

Hays, Peter L. "Biblical Perversions in *Desire under the Elms.*" *Modern Drama,* XI (February 1969), 423–428.

Herbert, Edward T. "Eugene O'Neill: An Evaluation by Fellow Playwrights." *Modern Drama,* VI (December 1963), 239–240.

Hinden, Michael. *"The Birth of Tragedy* and *The Great God Brown." Modern Drama,* XVI (September 1973), 129–140.

Holtan, Orley I. "Eugene O'Neill and the Death of the 'Covenant.' " *Quarterly Journal of Speech,* LVI (October 1970), 256–263.

Keane, Christopher. "Blake and O'Neill: A Prophecy." *Blake Studies,* II (Spring 1970), 23–34.

Krutch, Joseph Wood. "O'Neill's Tragic Sense." *American Scholar,* XVI (Summer 1947), 283–290.

LaBelle, Maurice M. "Dionysus and Despair: The Influence of Nietzsche upon O'Neill's Drama." *Educational Theatre Journal,* XXV (December 1973), 436–442.

Lecky, Eleazer. *"Ghosts* and *Mourning Becomes Electra:* Two Versions of Fate." *Arizona Quarterly,* XIII (Winter 1957), 320–338.

Lee, Robert C. "Eugene O'Neill's Remembrance: The Past Is the Present." *Arizona Quarterly,* XXIII (Winter 1967), 293–305.

————. "Evangelism and Anarchy in *The Iceman Cometh.*" *Modern Drama,* XII (September 1969), 173–186.

Leech, Clifford. "Eugene O'Neill and His Plays." *Critical Quarterly,* III (Autumn 1961), 242–256; III (Winter 1961), 339–353.

McAleer, John J. "Christ Symbolism in *Anna Christie.*" *Modern Drama,* IV (February 1962), 389–396.

Marcus, Mordecai. "Eugene O'Neill's Debt to Thoreau in *A Touch of the Poet.*" *Journal of English and Germanic Philology,* LXII (April 1963), 270–279.

Metzger, Deena P. "Variations on a Theme: A Study of *Exiles* by James Joyce and *The Great God Brown* by Eugene O'Neill." *Modern Drama,* VIII (September 1965), 174–184.

Meyers, Jay Ronald. "O'Neill's Use of the Phèdre Legend in *Desire under the Elms.*" *Revue de Littérature Comparée,* XLI (January–March 1967), 120–125.

Mottram, Eric. "Men and Gods: A Study of Eugene O'Neill." *Encore,* X (September–October 1963), 26–44.

Muchnic, Helen. "Circe's Swine: Plays by Gorky and O'Neill." *Comparative Literature,* III (Spring 1951), 119–128.

Mullaly, Edward. "O'Neill and the Perfect Pattern." *Dalhousie Review,* LII (Winter 1972–1973), 603–610.

Myers, Henry Alonzo. *"Macbeth* and *The Iceman Cometh:* Equivalence and Ambivalence in Tragedy." *Tragedy: A View of Life.* Ithaca, N.Y.: Cornell University Press, 1956, 98–109.

Nethercot, Arthur H. "The Psychoanalyzing of Eugene O'Neill." *Modern Drama,* III (December 1960), 243–256; III (February 1961), 357–372.

————. "The Psychoanalyzing of Eugene O'Neill: Postscript." *Modern Drama,* VIII (September 1965), 150–155.

————. "The Psychoanalyzing of Eugene O'Neill: P.P.S." *Modern Drama,* XVI (June 1973), 35–48.

O'Neill, Joseph P., S.J. "The Tragic Theory of Eugene O'Neill." *Texas Studies in Literature and Language,* IV (Winter 1963), 481–498.

Pallette, Drew B. "O'Neill and the Comic Spirit." *Modern Drama,* III (December 1960), 273–279.

————. "O'Neill's *A Touch of the Poet* and His Other Last Plays," *Arizona Quarterly,* XIII (Winter 1957), 308–319.

Parks, Edd Winfield. "Eugene O'Neill's Quest." *Tulane Drama Review,* IV (March 1960), 99–107.

Pommer, Henry F. "The Mysticism of Eugene O'Neill." *Modern Drama,* IX (May 1966), 26–39.

Porter, Thomas E. "Puritan Ego and Freudian Unconscious: *Mourning Becomes Electra.*" *Myth and Modern American Drama.* Detroit: Wayne State University Press, 1969, 26–52.

Pratt, Norman T., Jr. "Aeschylus and O'Neill: Two Worlds." *Classical Journal,* LI (January 1956), 163–167.

Racey, Edgar F., Jr. "Myth as Tragic Structure in *Desire under the Elms.*" *Modern Drama,* V (May 1962), 42–46.

Raleigh, John Henry. "O'Neill's *Long Day's Journey into Night* and New England Irish-Catholicism." *Partisan Review,* XXVI (Fall 1959), 573–592.

Real, Jere. "The Brothel in O'Neill's *Mansions.*" *Modern Drama,* XII (February 1970), 383–389.

Reardon, William R. "O'Neill Since World War II: Critical Reception in New York." *Modern Drama,* X (December 1967), 289–299.

Redford, Grant H. "Dramatic Art Versus Autobiography: A Look at *Long Day's Journey into Night.*" *College English,* XXV (April 1964), 527–535.

Reinhardt, Nancy. "Formal Patterns in *The Iceman Cometh.*" *Modern Drama,* XVI (September 1973), 119–128.

Rosen, Kenneth M. "O'Neill's *Brown* and Wilde's *Gray.*" *Modern Drama,* XIII (February 1971), 347–355.

Rothenberg, Albert. "Autobiographical Drama: Strindberg and O'Neill." *Literature & Psychology,* XVII (Nos. 2–3, 1967), 95–114.

———, and Eugene D. Shapiro. "The Defense of Psychoanalysis in Literature: *Long Day's Journey into Night* and *A View from the Bridge.*" *Comparative Drama,* VII (Spring 1973), 51–67.

Roy, Emil. "The Archetypal Unity of Eugene O'Neill's Drama." *Comparative Drama,* III (Winter 1969–1970), 263–274.

———. "Eugene O'Neill's *The Emperor Jones* and *The Hairy Ape* as Mirror Plays." *Comparative Drama,* II (Spring 1968), 21–31.

———. "O'Neill's *Desire under the Elms* and Shakespeare's *King Lear.*" *Die Neueren Sprachen,* XV (January 1966), 1–6.

Rubinstein, Annette. "The Dark Journey of Eugene O'Neill." *Mainstream,* X (April 1957), 29–33.

Rust, R. Dilworth. "The Unity of O'Neill's *S. S. Glencairn.*" *American Literature*, XXXVII (November 1965), 280–290.

Skene, Reg. "*The Bacchae* of Euripides and *The Great God Brown.*" *Manitoba Arts Review*, X (Winter 1956), 55–65.

Sogliuzzo, A. Richard. "The Uses of the Mask in *The Great God Brown* and *Six Characters in Search of an Author.*" *Educational Theatre Journal*, XVIII (October 1966), 224–229.

Stafford, John. "Mourning Becomes America." *Texas Studies in Literature and Language*, III (Winter 1962), 549–556.

Stamm, Rudolf. "'Faithful Realism': Eugene O'Neill and the Problem of Style." *English Studies*, XL (August 1959), 242–250.

———. "The Orestes Theme in Three Plays by Eugene O'Neill, T. S. Eliot, and Jean-Paul Sartre." *English Studies*, XXX (October 1949), 244–255.

Stroupe, John H. "Eugene O'Neill and the Problem of Masking." *Lock Haven Review*, XII (1971), 71–80.

Thurman, William R. "Journey Into Night: Elements of Tragedy in Eugene O'Neill." *Quarterly Journal of Speech*, LII April 1966), 139–145.

Törnqvist, Egil. "Ibsen and O'Neill: A Study in Influence," *Scandinavian Studies*, XXXVII (August 1965), 211–235.

———. "Nietzsche and O'Neill: A Study of Affinity." *Orbis Litterarum*, XXIII (No. 2, 1968), 97–126.

———. "O'Neill's Lazarus: Dionysus and Christ." *American Literature*, XLI (January 1970), 543–554.

———. "Personal Nomenclature in the Plays of O'Neill." *Modern Drama*, VIII (February 1966), 362–373.

Trilling, Lionel. *Eugene O'Neill.*" *New Republic*, LXXXVIII (September 23, 1936), 176–179.

Valgemae, Mardi. "O'Neill and German Expressionism." *Modern Drama*, X (September 1967), 111–123.

Vena, Gary A. "The Role of the Prostitute in the Plays of Eugene O'Neill." *Drama Critique*, X (Fall 1967), 129–137; XI (Winter 1968), 9–14; XI (Spring 1968), 82–88.

Vincent, W. Ernest. "Five Electras—Aeschylus to Sartre." *Southern Speech Journal*, XXIV (Summer 1959), 225–235.

von Hofmannsthal, Hugo. "Eugene O'Neill," tr. Barrett Clark. *The Freeman*, VII (March 21, 1923), 39–41.

Waith, Eugene M. "Eugene O'Neill: An Exercise in Unmasking." *Educational Theatre Journal*, XIII (October 1961), 182–191.

Walton, Ivan H. "Eugene O'Neill and the Folklore and Folkways of the Sea." *Western Folklore,* XIV (July 1955), 153–169.

Whitman, Robert F. "O'Neill's Search for 'A Language of the Theatre.'" *Quarterly Journal of Speech,* XLVI (April 1960), 153–170.

Winchester, Otis W. "History in Literature: Eugene O'Neill's *Strange Interlude* as a Transcript of America in the 1920's." *Literature and History,* ed. I. E. Cadenhead, Jr. Tulsa, Okla.: University of Tulsa, 1970, 43–58.

Winther, Sophus Keith. *"Desire under the Elms:* A Modern Tragedy." *Modern Drama,* III (December 1960), 326–332.

————. "Eugene O'Neill—The Dreamer Confronts His Dream." *Arizona Quarterly,* XXI (Autumn 1965), 221–233.

————. "O'Neill's Tragic Themes: *Long Day's Journey into Night." Arizona Quarterly,* XIII (Winter 1957), 295–307.

————. "Strindberg and O'Neill: A Study of Influence." *Scandinavian Studies,* XXXI (August 1959), 103–120.

Wright, Robert C. "O'Neill's Universalizing Technique in *The Iceman Cometh." Modern Drama,* VIII (May 1965), 1–11.

Catalog

If you are interested in a list of fine Paperback
books, covering a wide range of subjects
and interests, send your name and address,
requesting your free catalog, to:

McGraw-Hill Paperbacks
1221 Avenue of Americas
New York, N.Y. 10020